*picked by Roz
(on advice of
Marj Monk)
Nov 14/05*

LAMBSQUARTERS

Scenes FROM

A *Handmade* LIFE

BARBARA M^cLEAN

RANDOM HOUSE CANADA

National Library of Canada Cataloguing in Publication Data

McLean, Barbara, 1949-
Lambsquarters: scenes from a handmade life

ISBN 0-679-31113-0

1. McLean, Barbara, 1949- 2. Farm life—Ontario—Grey (County)—
Anecdotes. 3. Grey (Ont. : County)—Anecdotes.
I. Title.

S522.C3M336 2002   C818'.603   C2001-903487-3

www.randomhouse.ca

Text design: CS Richardson

Printed and bound in the United States of America

10 9 8 7 6 5 4 3 2 1

For Thomas, Clare and Angus for roads taken.

And remembering J.B.

⤚ *Contents* ⤙

⤛ *LANDING* ⤜

⤙ MY FARM IS IN GREY COUNTY. A hawk circling improbably high above southern Ontario sees a land mass bordered on the north by Georgian Bay, the west by Lake Huron and Lake St. Clair, the south by Lake Erie, and the east by Lake Ontario and Lake Simcoe. Facing west, the hawk sees the shape of an animal in the land below, the tail heading up the Bruce Peninsula, the feet treading on Niagara Falls and Haliburton, the forehead etched by the St. Clair River, and the trunk, for this is clearly an elephant, nuzzling the cities of Windsor and Detroit.

As the hawk's spirals tighten, his path circles south central Ontario, and he skirts the flank of the elephant. His elevation decreases, and he is visible overhead from my farm, first as a speck and then recognizable, his tail fanned out, his belly streaked and his wings tipped dark. He catches good thermals over the Dundalk Plain.

When he dives for a deer mouse in my hayfield, the hawk lands, briefly, over the womb of the elephant. It is a vast open space, isolated from other farms and cushioned by soft hills and gentle valleys. It is where we came to incubate as a couple and apprentice to be stewards of the land.

WE ARRIVED HERE in our early twenties by way of the city. Thomas was right out of medical school and keen to start a country practice in the nearby town of Murphy's Mill. I would take on the house, the land, the creation of a life in the country. The area had been designated as medically under-serviced, and the province guaranteed an income if we stayed for four years. The land provided rich soil to extend roots, dig in and stay. Murphy's Mill is treed and spired, a road winding in from the south like a Carrington painting or a Maud Lewis. A farming town with feed stores and equipment dealers, it is far enough from the city to have a life of its own.

It was autumn when we first saw it. The maples had sucked in their sap and turned. Fuchsia and gold, vermilion and amber against the deep greens of pines and cedars. We were shown property throughout the area surrounding Murphy's Mill, toward Lewiston and Adieu, to Coppice and Nunn, Trustful and Beeton, but we settled on a farm near the village of Alderney.

At the time I didn't know we would need it: community. My quest was for land, a house, a barn, hills and grass and rocks we could call our own, shape into something with our hands, our strong backs and our dreams. The rest seemed peripheral, irrelevant, separate. My focus was small, personal, tight.

I saw a picture first. In the realtor's window. An old brick farmhouse set in a grove of thick lilac and maple. The photo was blurry but revealing, like a silhouette of grandeur superimposed on a double negative. Old Ontario cottage style, local brick, centre dormer with failing gingerbread trim, solid front door, stone steps askew, ancient gardens overgrown. Twenty-three acres—ten workable—house, barn and drive shed. Unimproved, affordable.

I crossed my fingers. Both hands. The middle digits stretching outward over the next two. My reflex for luck or for lying. I can tuck them up into fists so nobody sees, as I did at my wedding, fearful of pledging medieval and unkeepable vows.

By the time we got close to the house I was disoriented from a rabbit-chase ride through the country, viewing every farm-for-sale from the back seat of the car. But emerging from the canopied concession, over the dusty railway tracks marked with a white X and up the esker, I caught a glimpse of the nineteenth century on the far hill.

From the high land to the west was a clear view of the house, perched alone across the valley. The cedars were lower then, and the house profiled south, its top window peaked by dormer angles, its brick bleached austere against the rich colours of October maples front and back. I remember the barn, which was a step behind, bashful, of serviceable grey weathered board. Its roof fugued the perfect pitch of the house.

I locked my eyes on the farmstead until trees intervened. Roadside elm and aspen tangled with grapevine, elderberry and chokecherry, and the tamarack rose from the marsh. At the hill's crest the house came into view again, solid now, straight-eyed to the road. Two first floor windows stared, equidistant from the central entrance beneath the dormer. A square-shouldered house, tattered, battered, in want of attention, poor but proud.

The autumn lilacs crowded around both sides of the house and tapered off down the fencerows. Fair trees of lilacs, almost as high as the house itself. And apple trees as old as the bricks of the house filled the front orchard, their meadow ploughed around them, brown earth after a harvest of mangels. The ploughshare had reprieved the perennials. They sprouted stubbornly from the grass and weeds. A wash of rosehips dripped off untrimmed bushes.

The house looked untouched. No aluminum doors, aerials, angel stone. No dog barking or sleeping. No swing. The side door, off its hinges, angled into a decrepit back kitchen. There were treacherous holes in the floor, and grey and maroon flowered linoleum covered the stronger boards. One wall was plastered and wainscotted in wide beaded pine—remnants of former care in a space for warm-weather preserving, churning and feasting. The few windows were opaque with grime, cobwebs and fragments of curtain so worn they would tear if ten flies landed on them.

Inside the house proper, things improved and worsened. Intact floors, walls and ceilings flashed the paint and debris of the reclusive former tenant in a skirmish of odour and pattern, colour and dirt. His shelter? Two rooms: the kitchen, a complete winter bedsit with woodstove, and one tiny upper bedroom for summer sleeping.

A pantry offered a shallow enamel sink that had once been white, a cold water tap from the well, and a hand pump connected to the cellar cistern, which filled with rainwater through a downspout from the roof. That was the water supply in the house. Well, there was a toilet in the upstairs hall too. But no basin there, no hot water tank, no shower or bath. There was electricity. The house had been wired in the 1940s and had just enough power for the few light bulbs dangling bare from the ceilings. Forty amps for house and barn.

Treacherous oil-burning stoves were rusting away in the living room and back kitchen, but the only reliable heat radiated from the wood cookstove. White and black, with a reservoir, its pipes going straight through the ceiling to the occupied bedroom, and bending through the wall to finger heat into the next room, and out a buttressed chimney. Each downstairs ceiling had chimney and heat holes so that pipes could meander throughout the house, and heat could rise through intricate iron plates over what our then unborn children would come to call their holler holes.

The parlour was wedged shut. Disuse had warped the doors and roller-coastered the floor. The boards had heaved like rocks from frost, swelled from damp, buckled from humidity and were now resigned to abject neglect. Like the other unused rooms, the parlour was empty. No furniture to disimagine, no camouflage to interpret, no fancy dressing, just bare walls, floor, ceiling, and puttyless windows blotted out with homemade storms of plastic and wood, trapping millions of flies and years of dust. The place was almost derelict. A brick tent. With outbuildings.

At the barn, boards were loose, soffits missing and roof panels lifting, but the weather was still on the outside. Two lofts with ladders, ropes and pulleys for ancient hayloads, hinged doors toeing in, and a granary lined in tin. The stable was a warren of rabbit pens stacked on rugged cattle stanchions, and the chains of former Jerseys and Holsteins who once gave up their milk. Their spirits seemed to linger, lying heavy and still.

A privy, its trench filled in, its seat gone, hadn't even a half-moon in its door. It leaned against the drive-shed, a long low building with iron bars hooking the front to the back, a pole frame and a dirt floor. It housed an implement I couldn't name then, painted red, picked out in black and gold—a seed drill, I know now—as well as tanks and barrels, spiles and sap buckets that were battered and worn and mended with lead. Beyond the drive-shed, forming its end wall, was the pioneer shelter. A log house, rotting, its chinking shattering and shrinking, falling to the ground.

I saw no rot that day. I breathed in only the air of possibility, of recovery, of stability and future. The rusty roof, the missing glass, the tilts and angles of slipping foundations and ill-fitting hardware misted out of focus behind the vast sense of impending connection and claim from, and for, this place.

From the first moment it became clear. Together, Thomas and I would become stewards and careful guardians of a property that dreams are made on. Its history was a vast effort of human hope, labour, tenacity, frustration and love. Woods and fields, hills and valleys, swamp and dry land were to be protected and nurtured in our naive hands. It would be our first and only foreseeable home, where we would learn about each other, about farming, about everything that would make us who we are. We didn't know then that we would conceive our children here and raise them with lambs and chicks and flowers, and fruit from trees that were planted before any of us drew breath. We only knew we wanted to turn this shell into a home and make it ours.

⊰ *BUS ROAD* ⊱

THE REAL ESTATE AGENT claimed it was a good road to buy on. A school bus road. The snowplough opens it early each day in the winter. "You'll be able to get out," he said.

We had no concept of the local climate. We couldn't picture snowbanks devouring the road, covered now with the brilliance of falling autumn leaves. Our attention was on the house, the barn, the huge task of taking on this place. Getting out was the least of our worries. Buses didn't figure.

⋘ *HOUSE* ⋙

➢ I'D NEVER SIGNED a cheque with the word "thousand" on it before. My hand shook. The bank had lent the money, we drew up the documents and the deed was ours. Joint owners.

It was October, and the leaves were falling, the sky greying, the earth closing down. Fields were ploughed or browning with late corn. Frosted flowers rotted on soft stems, or were flattened, or bravely held up seed pods for those confusing fall warblers Peterson calls "troublemakers."

The house was so empty. Echoes met us, then hid behind walls, around corners and disappeared. Generations of one family had lived here. Born and died within the walls. They had sold out for a song to a rabbity bachelor only ten years before. Would their ghosts accept our tenancy?

All I could manage was to walk from stark room to

room, up and down stairs, in and out the various doors and start over again. Dizzy from circling, listing from the slant in the floors, overcome with the responsibility of ownership.

Neighbours arrived. They farmed to the north and the east. Shared line fences. Good fences. They had small kids and large dogs. Fast tractors and slow schedules. They sent their son to lure us over, so they could check us out and see for themselves. They took us in for tea and tales.

With their welcome came their warning, the first of many. October was waning toward Hallowe'en, they cautioned, when local goblins and hooligans set fires and smashed glass. So we came prepared with sleeping bags, dog, flashlights and candy, and waited on the darkest of nights for vandals to appear. For the privy to be tipped, the windows soaped, the barn burnt. We were city people then. With city people's fears. But we got only a couple of carfuls of kids—out here the spaces are too great to walk. We filled their bags with treats, admired their disguises, listened as the gravel crunched when they drove away. Such dark. Such silence.

We slept in the west bedroom because it seemed contained and whole. The wallpaper, painted a dull blue, was bubbling, but not hanging in strips. There were no mouse holes in the baseboards, and the window seemed secure. We slept on the floor with the dog at our feet, camping with a real roof over our heads. Our roof.

The kitchen seemed vast in the morning, linoleumed, and wainscotted in thin board painted to look like tile. Black with white lines. We had a couch, a small electric two-burner stove and an antique fridge, which had all been left behind. And we had the wood stove, stoked from the cooling coals of the night before. We wore our coats until it warmed, brewed our coffee and tea, made toast over the open flame and looked at each other in wonder.

When I pulled on my boots they were full of kibble. All night the mice had been busy stowing it away from the dog's bowl, amazed at their find. I up-tipped every boot for years after.

Outside in the frost I dug away at resistant soil, rocky soil, rooted soil, and planted a hundred daffodils in the geriatric orchard. That might have been my first attempt to focus. To concentrate on something small so as not to be overwhelmed by the enormity of the work to be done. The whole house. And the barn. And the shed. The fences and fields and woodlot. Work for ever.

We were loath to hire anyone to do anything we thought we could manage. We'd just returned from Greece, where plaster is rough. We were acquainted with paint. We didn't seek perfection.

I scraped layers of wallpaper until my wrists were jammed and my fingertips raw. Took great delight in any piece that exceeded postage-stamp size. Lived in a slurry of hot steam and old glue, stuck to the stairs as I tried to move higher in the hall, a slow step at a time, the walls getting bigger and higher as the paper refused to budge. Seven layers, and if I scraped too hard I gouged the wall. A loathsome job, to be repeated in every room in the house. Inch by inch.

We spent all our free fall weekends here, driving the hundred miles from Lake Simcoe where Thomas worked as a locum in a general practice until the move. We packed our car each weekend with some comfort to add to the house. A two-dollar chair, a three-dollar cupboard. Pieces picked up at wreckers or auctions. Salvage from garbage piles and dumps. We were scavengers and finders, and I spent my weekdays designing, scheming, dreaming and planning, stripping my finds, my treasures. Re-covering and painting, varnishing and polishing. Turning early straw into gold. Then finally the solstice arrived, the season shifted and winter fell. In sheets of ice and blankets of snow, we packed the last load in the car, filled the rented truck with our eclectic chattels and braved the storm.

Snow swirled through the fields as we arrived. It filled the lane and buried the doorways. Our Dutch-born neighbour tractored in, scraped a path for our truck with astounding speed. We dubbed him *de vliegende Hollander*—the flying Dutchman.

So little work had been done. The firms we hired

to heat and plumb, to wire and stabilize all blamed each other for their truancy: until the cement floor was poured there could be no furnace; without heat the cement wouldn't cure. And it went on. So we found ourselves in January with little heat, no hot water, few lights. The tradesmen would drop in, leave their tools and not return for a week at a time. I wore more and more wool and scraped away alone at my endless walls, bravely trying to avoid despair during the long days as Thomas set up his practice in Murphy's Mill. Many days I did not succeed.

WE AWOKE to the cold each morning. Thomas would light the stove before leaving for town. His practice was instantly busy; the whole neighbourhood became patients. And I scraped and plastered, scrubbed and painted, demolished and rebuilt. I was contained in these walls I wanted to love. I had no transportation. I had no friends. And there was nowhere I could sit for a moment with my tea or my book and not be overwhelmed by the work to be done.

IT WAS DIFFICULT to get clean. Thomas showered at the hospital, and sent out his shirts. There was no laundry in town, but the dry-cleaning woman did them herself. I was stuck. Like the pioneers before me, I had only the water I could heat and the vessels I could find to bathe in. The reservoir in the woodstove filled a plastic baby bath to sit in, a bucket for my feet, and saucepans for my hands, one on each side. Too much of me was exposed to the wind from unstormed windows, leaky doors. And getting out was awkward. And as cold as church.

MONTHS PASSED BEFORE WATER RAN hot in the taps, before the iron bath was heaved up the stairs, before the sinks went in and heat blew through virgin pipes. Workmen came and went, intruded on my space or left me waiting desperately for their help, neither state a comfort. They mocked my plastering, questioned my judgment, laughed at my mistakes. The work took its toll, though I was young and strong.

I learned to focus. To home in on detail. To complete one small task after another. To learn my farmhouse board by board, wall by wall, window by window until I could venture out beyond its doors and begin to work the land around it.

⤙ *FARMYARD* ⤚

⫽⫽ THAT SPRING, BEFORE the first snowdrop was
planted, before the crocus spread and the scilla grew its
six heads, I emerged from the house to mud, weeds and
flaws throughout the demesne. In front of the house
was a ploughed mess oozing earthworms and snails,
sprouting dandelions and burdock, which for years I
hopefully mistook for rhubarb.

Fences I'd stared through like windows in the fall
suddenly caught my eye. They were rough and rusting,
too frail to hold anything out, keep anything in.
Raspberries in the back bred twitch grass with roots
reaching the next township. Water from everywhere
poured into the basement; its new concrete floor had
been carelessly installed with the drain at the high point.
We seemed to hold the headwaters of a whole river system
in our dank cellar.

The neighbour advised permanent pasture for the

front, and though I was skeptical at first, I now per-
ceive its merits. The mix of legume and grass, clover
and fescue, timothy and rye thrive together when the
weather is fair, but divide the responsibility to be
green when it's not. Some plants suffer in drought but
relish the floods, while others wither with insects but
fight off the weeds.

The area challenged my rake and hoe. Clods from
the plough lay furrowed like forks in a drawer. Hillocks
of hardpan were sprinkled with stone. I did get through
it, arms aching and filthy. I hacked and I trampled,
smoothed and spread, then set my pace, seed bag slung
over my shoulder, walking that walk I'd seen only in a
Millet painting of a peasant seeding the land. I found
my rhythm.

Green grew, and grows, mixed with all the flowers
that flew in at the time and have since. *Taraxacum
officinale*, the lowly dandelion, competed with newly
feathered goldfinches for brightness on the ground,
and white clover globes shone through the green like
miniature bulbs of light. Purple charlies crept.

Perennials dotted the edges. Plants I had no names
for then, but slowly learned to read, to tend, to antic-
ipate from year to year. When the grass grew I cut
around them, leaving clumps on the lawn like relief on
a painting, like lumps in gravy, sadly neglected flowers, left to live by their wits. I wonder how many I
missed, clipped with the grass and lost forever in the

days before order was established and beauty could be cultivated.

I tackled the raspberries growing in a tangle behind the house. Just a couple of rows filled with leaves, trellised on grass, rusting away from neglect. It took gloves and boots, thick denim and canvas to enter their slum. Wool sweaters stuck to the canes like fleece to barbed wire, and thorns penetrated every soft surface. The canes thwacked my face when I got them loose, and scraped my wrists, the only flesh exposed. I looked like the loser in a cat fight when it was over and the patch was no winner. With great spaces of void, then massed clumps of cane, the patch was a wild mess that spring.

I learned about speed. About the slow pace of late spring, when work was delayed by rain and mud, when the ground could not be worked or even traversed. Then the sudden sun and the rush to plant, to dig out the clods and rake and scatter in a fury, the soil drying by the minute, threatening to harden to stone. Work unceasing, bones weary at the end of long light-filled days, muscles stiffening, skin browning, my face weathering and taking on the look of the land itself, early hints of furrows to come.

We planted little at first. A few potatoes, bought from a bin at the general store in Alderney, and peas, beans, carrots and lettuce. They paralleled the raspberries in sickly rows, shadowed by the giant maple to the west. I learned from books or neighbours' nudges:

soak the beans overnight; cut the potatoes with three eyes in each piece for planting; use apple tree prunings to support the peas; sow lettuce every two weeks.

Though our crop grew slowly, our pasture jumped. Waves of orchard grass beyond the sagging fence headed up too soon. The timothy lagged behind, and the thistle and burdock awaited their chance, hovering at the fencerow, intent to invade. The pasture was out of control in a flash, beyond the level we could mow or maintain, and we were not ready for livestock of our own to chew it into submission.

The neighbour brought cattle, steers and heifers, I believe. Crossed Hereford on Holstein, black with white faces, roast beef on the hoof. They lapped sheaves of grass with raspy tongues, cut the field into tussock and turf. They ruminated at dusk, lowed at night, high-kicked at dawn, frisky for another day of grazing away from home. In moonlight their faces shone from the field like disembodied ghosts, their jaws circling, their eyes half-closed in bovine thought. They brought manure and flies, great plops of cow pies, and I found these cattlebeasts immense and frightening, their playful curiosity overshadowed by their drooling tongues, their manure-flicking tails, their great cleft hoofs.

They spurred us to clean out the barn and find flocks of our own. We filled truckloads with rubbish, fed bonfires with junk, forked barrows full of dung from decades of stock. Board by board we heaved and sorted, cutting our bare arms on wire and mesh, bruising our bodies with trips over stanchions, with wrenching square nails from their homes in thick beams. I coated rusty steel with bright white and paint-ed the barn doors red from my childhood dreams, where all barns glowed red and white. We discovered the windows, scraped off the grime, replaced the lights and illuminated even more debris. Rolling up our sleeves we kept digging and ripping, dragging and hauling until we had a space, some pens, some possibility of use.

In our early days we had travelled through Scotland, Ireland and Greece. We had swept spots of moor clean of droppings for our tent, heard the odd bleating of a sleeping lamb, the snore of its dam, the rustle of fleecy bodies shifting and succumbing to sleep. Sheep entered our dreams then and we had stored them away, fluffy gauze, in woolen moments of meditation. They were clouds, drifting between rational thoughts, but they surfaced now as solid mat-ter, as the text to write a life on.

We put the word out. We wanted sheep.

⊶ *BUS RECRUITS* ⊷

A KNOCK AT THE DOOR. A strange woman, smiling. "Will you have any kids on the bus this September?" Kids? Me? Us? I wonder now about that visit. I have no idea who she was or whether she really went from door to door to find filling for the great cheese-coloured bus that ran down our road each day. But no, no kids for the bus. Not this year. Likely not ever.

⤙ *PAGE WIRE* ⤚

⫷ BEFORE WE PLANTED GRASS, we fenced in
the mangel field. Or fenced out. It was difficult to
know whether the clods of earth, menacing and dark,
were a danger or a lure. Wire loops, rusting with age,
creaking with dry, hobbled and loped against failing
posts, waved in winds and leaned with snow. The raspberries twisted through their own wire mess, which
blended into the barnyard's tall untended herbage,
camouflage for ground-loving beasts.

Barbed wire sagged at the top of the meadow, three
useless strands for the itinerate cattle to tease. The fence
worked for our first summer, but we hated the thought
of its cruel pricks and spent hours that fall rolling it up
into rusty balls, like huge medieval weapons, and carrying them off to the dump. The side field in front of the
barn had no fence at all, was just lumped in together
with the lane, the barnyard, anywhere the farm's former

animals had wanted to roam. So Thomas learned to fence. As he got to know the back roads and lanes throughout the townships while on house calls, he watched the neighbours, took mental notes, made patterns in his head. He asked questions, gathered advice.

The mill keeper in Alderney sold us the materials and lent us the fence stretcher. We learned about rods, those units of measurement that had disappeared from our lives after elementary school, and from everywhere else in the world but the local mill, as far as we knew. One rod equals 5 1/2 yards, or 5.03 metres, and the plural isn't used around here, so we needed twenty rod of fence. Page wire, they call it, a mesh of rectangles, each about the size of a salt block, smaller sections at the bottom to keep lambs in, predators out.

I watched Thomas measure the distance. Some unconscious knowledge overtook his body as he walked with giant strides; intuitively he knew each to be a yard. Playing grown-up Mother May I. He also knew how to dig. I'd never seen him dig before. We'd never owned a spade. But the work came to him brilliantly. A natural digger. And I've hardly seen him without a shovel nearby since. He carries one in the back of the truck for roadside raids—discount trees and shrubs, ditch lilies.

We didn't have a truck that first summer, so we used the car, a little black Vauxhall of pre-seatbelt vintage, to try to stretch the fence. The posts were all in. We had cut them all to length from the cedar in the bush and gently placed them in three-foot holes. Three-foot holes. I can write that in a second, but the effort it took to dig even one of those holes would take pages.

The page wire was attached at the north end, a few staples held it along the way, and the fence stretcher waited at the roadside, joined by a chain to the back of the car. I might have done it the other way round, pulled from south to north unobserved, but gravity defied the magnet. We were soon discovered, and the flying Dutchman was there in a flash. Why didn't we call him? Why did we think we could do this alone? He wheeled in the tractor (reverse his best gear), attached the fence and stretched it effortlessly. The mesh, trapped like Aphrodite by Hephaestus, was suddenly wanton and weak to its iron strength.

We pounded in staples, ten to a post, posts placed every eight feet. And the corners braced. An angled post, notched to the ends in one direction, reinforced in the other with twisted number nine wire, the farmer's friend. And the corner post was a bully, a thick tough beast, engineered to last, to hold its own and others. The field lay fenced, from barn to road, shiny and sprightly and straight. Only the post-tops stood askew, and, in those days before the chainsaw, needed personal attention. They were hand-sawn on an angle to deflect the snow and sheer off the rain. The tips lined up in the sights in a near perfect trail down the paddock for birds to perch on until the sheep arrived to claim the space.

✂ *LAMBING* ✄

🐦 I WAS ROOTING AROUND, busy at some task one morning late that first summer, when I sensed a sleek navy Volvo glide in the lane. We knew a few neighbours by then, had put out the word, had asked for sheep. Willis Harris, limping from arthritic knees that predated arthroscopy and replacement, unpacked himself from the passenger seat of the strange car, his red hair vying with his red face for brilliance, his lips split from too much sun, his hands gnarled like yellow birches growing on granite. He probably hadn't ridden in anything but a truck or tractor for years, maybe for ever.

He wore green, the farmer's uniform, dirty and mussed from the morning's chores, but no doubt well clean hours before. He kept his hat on. We'd asked him about sheep, had seen his flock by the road, but no, he had said, they were just old yoes from the west, just to keep the grass down at the far farm, there's nothing we'd want from them. R.F. Harrow, he said, was our man.

And now here they were together in Mr. Harrow's car, to look at the farm and suss me out as a potential shepherd. A gentle man, cultured, Mr. Harrow wore neat khaki pants, pleat-pressed, and a cap with a peak. His eyes made his denim shirt look blue. He shook my hand firmly, his own uncalloused. He wore Wallabees, not work boots. Not a speck of dirt on him or the car. I showed them my hen, Mrs. Chicken, and her chicks, cooped in the yard in a makeshift house. And I remember feeling foolish, playing at animals around these serious men who made farming their life.

But my sincerity must have shown, for Mr. Harrow sold us some sheep. The last of his Hampshire cross Suffolk flock, a black-faced breed on strong black legs, with wool springy and dense and short. We put the sheep in pens and found them a ram and learned everything we could about how to keep them.

I read widely, from the *TV Vet*, which I still hide behind the door frame of my grandmother's glassed-in bookshelf (the book's spine is a garish orange and turquoise), to academic veterinary texts, to farmer's manuals and magazines. I apprenticed in neighbours' barns for births and shearings; I sat in on agricultural courses at college and learned to manage my small flock well.

There were only five ewes that first year, all pre-named. Old Spot, Hampy, Blackie, Susie and Maggie.

Ramsey was the first ram, a thrifty Suffolk lamb, and though he was inexperienced, he performed like a professional and every dam "caught."

I remember the first year's lambing. It began during the biggest snowstorm of the season, on April 3rd, back when we measured in inches—we got a full twenty-one. The age-of-majority snowstorm. There wasn't just snow, which can be moved, but wind, which moves for you. The snow was light—too light to walk on. I sank to my hips in the path from house to barn. And I walked that path day and night, watching and waiting for a first new breath. I had seen lambs born in other barns, had read of their birth, knew what to expect. But I had not been responsible.

Each time I inspected the barn, the wind took my tracks. I thought of farmers lost between barn and house, found when the storm was over. I thought of stringing a rope. But this is Ontario, not the prairies, and my journey was short. Nevertheless, I was alone for three days. Thomas, caught in town when the storm hit, was warm at the hospital, tending the sick. Three frightening days when no one could move, either in or out. I read of multiple births, retained placentas, prolapses, breaches, head-out-and-swollen presentations, head-back presentations, tail presentations, disasters. For three days I had no human contact as I awaited my first delivery. I was a nervous midwife.

It took bulldozers to dig out the road that year. In

April. Cruel indeed. But the first lamb, when it came, neither malpresented nor worried. It was born in twenty minutes, was up and sucking in seconds. A perfect male, and I called him Virgil and sing of him now.

A ewe in labour wants to be alone. Garbo. This one found a corner in the barn, walked around in circles like a dog remembering long grass, then began to paw the straw, making a nest. She arched her back a few times, circled a little more, pawed, and finally got down on her side. A few pushes, her neck stretched with the strain, and a small balloon appeared, full of fluid. Two feet, tiny points of hoofs, one slightly ahead of the other, white on the tips, shiny black further up.

A little furry wet nose appeared between the feet, the tongue out at the side and blue. Another push and the shape of the forehead was visible under the ewe's stretched skin, then through. The neck was so long, a swan emerging, followed by slowing shoulders, and the body slipped out with a small heave, a rush, a deluge of the sea it swam in.

Virgil, born to an elastic experienced ewe, came all of a sudden. Not precipitously, but predictably. Before he had a chance to cry, his mother chuckled to him. A low soft laughing bleat, like a short purr from an enormous cat, the communication of love from ewe to lamb. A lamb learns its mother's chuckle and answers. Out in the world now, covered in thick hot fluid and membrane, Virgil struggled to stand up, to find food.

His mother licked him off, fluffed his wool, trimmed his navel cord. He staggered, he splayed and finally he sucked.

I sat on the stable fence. An *accoucheur*.

IN THE EARLY YEARS, I was meticulous. I built little feeders for the nursery pens, wrote detailed descriptions of each lambing, stripped the dams' teats of their waxy plugs before the lambs got settled nursing, named each animal as it was born. Before a birth, in years without late snow, I would set up my chair in the barnyard and let the ewes mill around me. I'd put my hands on their bellies and feel the kicks, trace the outlines of the lives within them, burrowed deep beneath the wool. I'd live among them, frequently lying in the straw and sleeping with exhaustion after a long labour (Thomas off tending a human birth in Murphy's Mill), waking with the ewes' bleats in the middle of the night, helping when they needed help, watching when they did not.

I scrubbed empty pens with lye, brushed down every surface for every germ. I suffered losses as if they were my own; they were my own. They are still.

SHEEP HAVE A MOON of their own—estrus every eighteen or nineteen days of their season—but really they follow the sun. Only when the days get shorter do they ovulate. Their evolution has not caught up with their domestication. If they breed on short days, they lamb on long ones. And longer days are warmer days, and warmer days give stronger lambs.

In the last spring of the century, the barnyard was full of snow, the compost completely covered, the gates frozen open. The kitchen garden, moved now to a space south of the barn, was fast asleep, awaiting the runoff from the dark gold mine of manure, which was buried under its white duvet like a child in a dream, nescient to the life stirring within it, within the barn.

The first lamb is always a surprise. Some years it comes early, before I have a chance to fret; more often it is late, wearing me out before the event. I trudge to the barn to watch, to help, to marvel.

ONE BIRTH, on day four or five, could have been disastrous. The first lamb was born easily, the mother attentive. She was so attuned to the first, she wouldn't go down to deliver the second. While she stood, it slipped out, supple and slinky in its thick wet membrane, and dropped to the ground encased in its caul like a sleek cabbage roll. I don't know how long a lamb can lie lifeless. I didn't stay on the fence to see. I cleared the membrane from its nose and mouth, encouraged it to breathe the clear air of the new world on this side of its bubble. It breathed. It shook. It started to life.

WHEN NEW, their ears are plastered back, stuck to the sides of their heads. As they dry off, the ears move forward, drooping from the weight of the birth fluids, the weight of the world. Sometimes it takes a day or so for the ears to perk, although lambs hear well, responding to their mothers' chuckles. Marking tags, small brass brads with numbers, tend to pull down the left ears for a few days, making them look a tad risqué. They are *fin de siècle* creatures, with body piercings, tattoos.

After an overnight with their dams in a mothering-up pen (a portable crib of hinged gates, four feet square) the new lambs meet in a central space. Then the bleating begins. Oh brave new world. And space. They can run, play, chase. But who are the other ewes? Are you my mother? Are you? Misrecognitions are met with bunts.

It is a fearful time, the move. A cacophony of chuckling mothers, bleating lambs, claiming calls. But the lambs learn their mums, their mates, new connections. This year, one has learned to steal. I recognize the thievery by the greasy wool on his forehead. Clearly he was grabbing a furtive suck from behind whenever he could and the wax from the udders was rubbing off on his head. A forensic certainty.

A ewe noses her lamb's backside when it sucks. If attentive, she will lift her body, arch her back to show the teat, offering it to the lamb. By sniffing, she identifies and encourages at the same time. If she has twins, she moves her head back and forth from one to the other, and if she has triplets, she will sometimes move away from a larger lamb and nose a smaller one in for a feed.

I remember Alfie, who was born to a reluctant mother in the late seventies. He was runty, only five or six pounds at birth, but he had a cocky constitution. When the ewes were lined up at the feeders, Alfie would go down the queue, sneaking a suck from each sheep in the row. The ewes would stamp their feet to detach him, but he'd get a bellyful by the end of the line.

THE END-OF-CENTURY TWINS, who to me were identical, were sorted and separated by their mother: one favoured, one a foundling. For five days I kept them penned in a tight space, waiting for the ewe to accept, to concede, to acquiesce to both. I was afraid she would reject and batter her ram lamb, who would grow up motherless in a barn full of mothers. He would have to rely on food from my bottle and would develop the barrel belly of the artificially fed. And I wondered about the scapegoat. The child who is not favoured. The distant part of the self pushed aside as too ugly, too frightening, too horrible to confront. The lamb of innocence thrust into the world of experience. The song of dissonance, its bleats unanswered.

⊷ *NAMING* ⊷

⊱ IT TOOK SOME TIME to name the farm. "Hi Lo," painted in dripping letters on the mailbox when we arrived, aptly described the terrain from corner to corner, but failed to capture our connection to the land. Perhaps we needed time to perfect our attachment, to meld with the dirt, rock and plants that were here and the animals and commitment we were to add.

A quarter of a farm, with lambs and weeds.

Lamb's quarters one of the names most commonly given to the widely diffused cosmopolitan weed, *Chenopodium album*, of the goosefoot family. . . . [An] erect, usually slender, much branched, pale green annual, 1 ft. to 10 ft. high, with somewhat lance-shaped, more or less lobed or toothed leaves, 1 in. to 4 in. long, commonly white-mealy beneath. . . . The young shoots of this plant are sometimes used as a pot-herb, like spinach. Lamb's quarters [is] also called pigweed. (*Britannica*)

Pigweed? Goosefoot? Lamb's quarters? This plant is a veritable menagerie of ovine, avian and swine. Lamb's quarters is a garden variety weed. So why did I name my farm after it? It was here, on disturbed ground. Ground that once felt the weight of soft moccasins, before being gouged by settlers in a past century, cleared and tilled into fat furrows. Shiny ploughshares followed faithful horses. Gee and haw over virgin terrain. The land grew complacent over the years. Fields were rotated and renewed, stooked with grain, planted in pasture, cut for hay. Gardens were tilled and tended. Roses, peonies, delphiniums, lilies. The bicolours of monkshood, and the vining sweet pea, emerging pink and white, but turning mauve then blue with age.

The vegetable patch fought against the sugar maple in the back yard, a garden edged with raspberries, asparagus and rhubarb planted in the full afternoon shade of the biggest tree on the land.

Lamb's quarters sprouted among the raspberry canes, sheltered by the tangle of fallen leaves, went to seed late and proliferated. The canes trapped weeds in a leghold and produced more prickles than fruit. Finally I cut them down, dug up the rhubarb, moved the asparagus and started a new kitchen patch just south of the barn. In the spring the lamb's quarters reappeared on the grave of the berries. Smaller, less bold, pale against the yellow green of new grass. Their seeds hitched a ride on the east wind and moved closer to the maple, between its gnarled feet where the blade can't go, around the doghouse in a palisade, against the fence.

You'd expect lamb's quarters to move in different circles, be a little exotic and frequent outdoor cafés. Cosmopolitan, erect, slender and lance-shaped, the mundane weed does a little goose step or a lamb gambol or a pigtail turn, holds its leaves at an angle, wears violet leafstick, and sports purple leaf-spots in spring. Like birthmarks on the newborn growing cycle, the spots harbinge the season and predict its mortality all at once. Liver spots of youth suggesting age. Irregular, deep hued or pale, these marks reflect the stalk lines, which feather the stem in subtle shading, mauve through purple to red. The lowly lamb's quarters has a natural variegation, a May blush for the picking.

THE LAND HERE was destined for sheep. And from sheep, lambs. Rolling, rocky, the fields and bog make perfect pasture, the cedar fencerows bountiful browse. When the grass thins and the sun wanes and the frost thickens on morning dew, the ewes gather around the ram pen, one or two or even three at a time, and make sheep eyes. The ram calls his throaty greeting, climbs front feet up the fence, schemes to get over, dreams like a ground-set lover with a mistress on a balcony. His hind legs are strong from dancing under the apple trees—the early Macs, the late Russets and York Imperials. Unable to wait for windfalls, he harvests the trees himself, reaching up on his back legs in a comic dress rehearsal for the real legwork of breeding in November.

His chance comes, the gates open and he pulls back his upper lip in a toothless grin, which serves, along with a chuckle and a sly ear nibble from behind, as his pickup line. He has little imagination or discrimination. The line is always the same. He is not subject to youth and beauty, coquetry and a down-turned lash. The ewes are all beautiful to him. He dances with them in turn, wanting each one to mother his babies.

And five months later they do. The barn, housing mothers and babes in a giant nursery, fills with the sweet bleats of lambkins. Mothering-up pens range in perfect order against the walls. A woolly barracks. Lamb's *quarters*.

When they leave the barn for pasture, the sheep find that gates and chutes lead to few choices for grazing, as this farm is not large. The standard hundred acres of the original tract was split early in the last century, and a quarter was severed off.

Lambsquarters named itself.

IN APRIL the renewing flock transforms the barn. Loose housing—big pens divided only by wooden gates—is rearranged every few days to accommodate the changing configurations of new mothers and lambs.

Sleep-deprived and short-tempered, I move slowly to that barn some mornings, stiff from kneeling over a difficult birth the night before, from bending under a ewe with a suckless lamb shivering from a midnight drop. I drag myself out of bed before dawn to check on my flock, help those in distress, feed the rest who are demanding their seasonal grain and molasses. The greedy ones brown their noses in the powdery sugar or choke on great mouthfuls of oats. The dog follows me to the Dutch door, hoping to slip into the barn where she will race up the stairs and send the cats to the top of the mow in a flurry of fur motes. The rooster crows-in the dawn, optimistic testimony to the morning's certain arrival, and summer pastures seem a distant wish, hiding under snow or muck or the pervasive grey of winter's end.

But May brings changes. Greening and preening, everything gears up to escape trapped winter spaces. Grass spears through the mud, legumes unfold, tree buds swell with juice and pulp until finally they burst, unfurl and test their fronds like new wings limp from the chrysalis. Early migrators land, hibernators wake, the tomcat misses meals. And young lambs, who've never even dreamed of grass, get their first taste. Like artichokes in balsamic vinegar, or asparagus in butter, the grass melts in their mouths, sparking virgin taste buds, calling perfect miniature hoofs to travel over this quarter farm to test out the endless salad on fence edge and borderline.

Weeds near rail fences have the best odds for full-gloried growth. If the rails are closely stacked, lamb's quarters can hide just out of the flock's reach and sprout between the posts. Occasionally a sheep will find enough room between the rails for its nose, then space to put its head through. It will munch its way to the pillory, get trapped and rarely think to retrace its route along the rails. Stuck in the stocks, it will tug and pull, dig in hind hoofs, shine the rail smooth with a lanolin neck, and bleat pitifully. The only way out is the way in, back where the rails were further apart. A handful of fresh greens will lure the sheep to freedom. Led by lamb's quarters to danger and back.

The ram, penned all summer in a paddock of his own, bounds to the garden gate on weeding days, begging for the mallows and grasses and lamb's quarters that I cull from the vegetable patch. With anchorous taproots, mallows are chained to the ground like Houdini. They break at the stem when I try to pull them out. Rarely do I turn the right combination and bring them up whole, but when I do, they're a feast for the tup and a triumph for the tiller. Twitch, crab and quack grasses have underground runners that travel over continents without stopping. But lamb's quarters, peppering the potato and pumpkin plants, are easy prey. Their roots are delicate and fibrous, and they jump out of the soil into my hands and into my ram. They leave friable earth in their wake; I can see where I've been.

⤙ *TENACITY* ⤚

🪶 A MOTHER HEN FUSSING, a hawk roosting, a dog with a bone. We expect animals to stay on track, to focus, to concentrate on survival. Attention deficit disorder is disallowed. Darwin in the barnyard.

My twin lambs are a combination of proton and electron, positive and negative. Named Alpha and Beta, called App and Ben for short. App is accepted, the lamb of her mother's life; Ben is bunted, marginalized. I look at him and think of the *Messiah*. For him the sad role, de-spis-ed, re-ject-ed, a lamb of sorrows and acquainted with grief.

Neither called nor answered, Ben wanders alone in a nursery of radiant mums and jubilant lamblings. If he approaches his mother's teat he is abandoned. She walks away, looking for her first-born, the darling. Afraid he will starve, I prepare a bottle. I expect to find him hunched, hungry, cold. I expect he will have given up, that he'll be pining from the abuse.

But Ben is tenacious. He is focused on eating, primed for surviving. If he is vigilant, he can approach his mother from behind to suck, but only when App is sucking from the front. I have never seen this configuration before. The attentive ewe, nuzzling the forward lamb, ignoring the backward. Can't she feel the pressure on both teats? Does she really not know?

For the milk to let down in a ewe, the lamb must bunt the udder. Not with a mere nudge, but with a vigorous punch from the pate. A large lamb will lift its mother right off her hind legs with the force. So Ben's backward move is not subtle. First he gives a pound, then he takes a pull. But as long as App is sucking in front, the ewe co-operates and allows Ben the hind teat. This isn't a quick suck and a calculated getaway. Ben is there for the duration. When lambs are young, their mothers stand still for minutes at a time to give them a continuous feed. Ben's mother stands politely, nosing App, talking to her, nudging her into the teat while Ben drinks from the rear. Usually twin lambs will settle on one side of their dam and not cross over. At this point, just a week after their birth, App and Ben are unsure of their territory. Sometimes App will reach through to the opposite side while Ben takes over, tail wagging, to finish what she's left.

A few days later and Ben strengthens. He is not as clean as the other lambs, since he must concentrate on the back end of his mother, but he is vigorous and growing. When he connects with the teat, he's a limpet—barnacle Ben.

Anything but stupid, sheep learn by example. A buddy has been watching Ben's antics and today I saw her imitate him. Ben was behind one side of his mother, and the unrelated lamb zipped in on the other. App, standing at the front, where a good lamb really belongs, was baffled to find no dinners left. She must have been connected first, for her mother would not feed only Ben. And the ewe clearly thought App was still on. She was nosing and nudging App, who was wagging her tail in anticipation and excitement (and frustration) while Ben and his friend were getting all the milk.

MANY MOTHERS are less than perfect. Our culture values only the vague concept of motherhood and offers little instruction in parenting. Sheep culture doesn't provide alternatives. If a ewe refuses to breast-feed, she doesn't have access to formula. Not by herself. An unfed lamb in the wild or in a hill flock would die. Attentive shepherds are like the Children's Aid: they round up lost souls and foster and protect them. But why is one mother kinder than another? Why favour one offspring more than the next?

It has been proven that a human baby recognizes its mother's scent, and will move toward it in a rudimentary way. If given an hour to lie naked against the mother's thigh, a newborn will slowly begin to move its legs. It will crawl to its mother's breast and attach itself, if we give it the chance, much as a lamb will find the teat. New lambs are awkward, splay-legged creatures, easily confused between front and back mother-legs, but their determination is boundless. Sheep mothers are there to help. They rise immediately after birth, offer the teats, lick off their newborns.

Bonding between human mothers and babies is sometimes more difficult. Women in labour have a history of being tied up, strapped down, rendered unconscious. We don't sniff; we gaze into eyes, we touch, we count body parts. We listen, we feel, we think about our connections. When human babies slither up their mothers' naked bellies with the cords still attached, and latch on to newly secreting breasts, the secrets of mother-love are released with the let-down of milk. But only babies can hear and taste them. The cord is cut, but the bond remains.

Or does it? Some mothers of twins manage football-holds on their babies, tucking one under each arm. The infants suck away in tandem. These mothers perfect a skill, nurse in record time, plop the full feedlings on their depleted chests, cross arms and burp one over each shoulder, lay them down in matching cribs, never needing to check the nail polish on the discreet toenail to tell them apart.

But for other mothers even one baby is a burden. They growl after the birth, turn to the wall. They prop the bottle and walk away. They shake, scream, hit, burn. We punish these mothers, having never supported them. We just expect them to know how to nurture. To have the mothering instinct. Collective unconscious. Primal knowledge.

YEARLING EWES make fragile mothers. They are teenagers, slight, sprightly, silly; they are often ill-equipped to settle with a lamb. Birthing may be difficult for them, or fairly quick, but they sometimes skitter, jump away from the birthing site, look around at their progeny in utter (and udder) disbelief. Mine? Are you serious?

These adolescent mums need tenacious lambs. They need lambs who have the will to win them over, bring them around to the idea of motherhood, of protection, of forgoing the freedom of lambhood to take on nurturing. It is a lot to ask. Even of a sheep. And some are not up to the task.

App and Ben's mother, despite her three lambings, had never raised twins. As a yearling, she loved her single lamb and was a nervous but competent mum. One late afternoon in the heart of spring, she was out on pasture and had found some soft new grass for a birthing bed. I brought her into the barn for protection, for attention. She and the lamb thrived and returned to the field proud and connected. The following year she lambed alone, overnight, unattended. While I slept, she gave birth to twins, the first a large lamb encased in a caul. It never breathed air.

I ran to the lifeless lump on the straw, reaching out to clear its airway, dreaming, like Mary Shelley, that I could rub it to life by the fire. But in its perfect package it was cold, slimy, dead. Neatly contained in a pellucid envelope, as beautifully wrapped as a Japanese present, this creature would provide no gift, be nobody's pet. I was glad for the healthy second lamb, although had it not arrived, the mother might have released the first from its silver cage, licked off its nose, pawed its back and chuckled it on.

With her history of raising only singletons, perhaps this ewe cannot conceptualize twins, even when they are conceived within her. All her lambs are alpha lambs. Firsts and onlies. But her beta lamb is not giving up. Little Ben struggles on, backwards, but moving ahead in his own tenacious struggle to reach some personal omega.

⤙ *LOFT* ⤚

⫷ MY FIRST RECOLLECTION of the word "loft"
is tangled in the attic of my grandparent's cottage. It
was a log house that Grandad had paid twenty-five dollars for and had moved to a piece of property he got by
trading an old car. It was only four logs high—they were
that thick. Big Timber Lodge, he called it.

Most of the cottage had no ceiling, just bare logs to
the eaves, then the beams and rafters inside the roof. But
on one end a second storey was framed, floored, railed
and laddered, but unwalled, open to the room below.
This was the loft. There were beds up there, but I was not
allowed to sleep in them. My grandfather died when I was
three. The cottage was sold. My memories are few.

I do recall being there—it must have been after his
death, before my grandmother sold it—and only
women were around. My mother, my grandmother,
perhaps my aunt and my sister—city women. Mice were

caught in a trap under the bed each night. And in the morning no one could touch them. I remember taking them by the tails and running outside, hurling them over the bank into the woods. Poor dead mice that no one else would bury. And I, a budding Antigone, covered them with leaves and regretted their deaths. Honoured their corpses.

I think my grandfather was a loft kind of person. I think he understood spaces apart and yet connected. He was a painter and a writer, and he appreciated children. On his mantel he carved, "Beside This Glowing Fire May Warmer Friendships Grow." He believed in fairies and Kipling and Dickens. And I regret his death. I regret not knowing him. But I treasure his paintings, his writings, his books. I visit his grave. And I carry his legacy in lofts.

When I first came to the farm—the day I saw it—I thought it had two lofts: one in the house and one in the barn. I don't know how long it took me to correct my terminology. In Grey County, the space above the stable is not a loft; it is a mow.

You mow (oh) hay when you cut it, but you put it in the mow (ou). The former is done low to the ground, and the second hurts, or houses owls. How helpful is phonics with the letters ow? Other places have haylofts, but here we have mows. In fact we have hay mows and straw mows, carved from the same space over the stable.

A mow in early June is an airy place. If the timing and season have been right, the mow will be all but empty, with a few bales of hay left perhaps, some old straw on top of the granary. All the beams are exposed, as well as the mortises and tenons, the hand-drilled holes holding hand-hewn rungs in the ladders to nowhere. Straight ladders go up either side from the middle. Suicide ladders that go almost to the roof and abruptly stop.

Light seeps in through the barnboards and throws diagonal rays across floors golden with strawdust or green with hayseed. Like Zeus morphing through the planks in a shower of gold to seduce Danae in her tower, the sun slides through the cracks to conceive a Perseus of its own in the promise of fodder to come. And rain on the metal roof first pings then escalates to a thunderous roar during a spring storm. There is little to absorb sound: Echo cries her lonely plea.

The barn was empty when we first came, of course. No animals; no feed. That first winter it stood forlorn and unvisited. The rusty siding and tin roof were its outward signs of grieving and loss. And during our first summer it lay lonely too. I learned about baling and stooking and mowing that summer, but not in my own barn. I helped fill the neighbours' mow with my hay in return for their knowledge. Books can't convey the heat in the hay mow when the crop reaches the top, or the height of the wagon and thrill of riding on a well packed load from the field. Sweating from working the land, bitten by cut stalks and thistles, I flexed my aching back and extended my weary arms.

The second year, I turned my barn loft into mows, one for hay and one for straw. I had my first sheep now, just a few, but they were resident. They would winter here, would need feed. The crop came in, abundant, dry, a little later than I would learn to like, but wholesome and good. We got the elevator set up: a long conveyor belt (just a little wider than a bale of hay) tilting from the barn bank through the door and across the barn floor to reach the highest mow. Until the haystack began to grow, the elevator just picked up the bales to drop them on the floor, a senseless operation. I knew now how to pack my mow with tight bales on the outside row, to build a wall of hay that would withstand the winter climbing. A reticulated wall, like the second stomach of a sheep (called the reticulum or honeycomb bag) where it was headed. We set up each row in the opposite direction—now lengthwise, now widthwise—for strength and safety. When a boot hit a crease between the bales mid-winter, the foot would just sink down to the knee, not forever.

The ladder came to life as the day progressed. Climbing was easy as the bales came in, just a row at a time. But getting down to the barn floor for lemonade between loads could only be done on those ancient rungs, set on the outer edge of the haystack, like a rock face, a perpendicular decline. As the wall grew, the trip got more treacherous, extending beyond the ladder's top, over the high beam, where there were no guardrails or ropes or carabiners. No crampons on my boots. My cottage loft had not prepared me for this. It had been small and safe, but I had been taught to fear it. Perhaps that fear festered and was now resurfacing.

I still resist the high hay mow on the first cold days of winter feeding, when I'm alone all day, where no one would find me if I lost my footing and fell. The sheep would bleat to be fed, but help wouldn't hear.

The straw mow is smaller, beside and over the granary, which has pronunciation problems of its own. Grain fills it, but it loses the hard *a*-sound in the process and ignores the single *n*. Granary rhymes with tannery. Archaic words for archaic practices that go on all around us still if we will see. The straw mow fills itself. The golden bales are so light and dry they can be tossed gently into place. The straw gilds the mow and closes in both sides with living walls of bedding and feed. Gold and green. Echo, shamed and rejected as in the myth, disappears across the fields to the edge of the wood as long as the barn is full.

THE HOUSE LOFT is still a loft, but changed too in its way. We first discovered it behind a derelict door, which revealed a forgotten staircase, unlighted, leading narrowly through unfinished walls. Dried plaster oozed from slatted lath on one side; you could see the blackish insides of outdoor boards on the other. On a spacer between the two-by-fours was a mummified mouse. A bit big for a mouse. A mere case of a rodent, tanned from inside out, leathern and brown, the grey fur lost in its dry preservation. The stairs were decidedly steep, though not perpendicular like the barn ladders, and led directly to a dark sleeping loft, fallen into disrepair from neglect, over the back kitchen.

Mysteriously, nothing about the loft was quite finished. There were no walls or floor or ceiling, but loose boards left lying over the joists made hunched walking possible around the open stairwell. One small window graced—no it did not grace, it punctured the dormer end. The glass was cracked, fly-specked, cobwebbed, opaqued with years of disinterest.

I don't know if we were told it was a sleeping loft or if I invented that use for generations of grandchildren, farmhands, and summer visitors who were brave or disrespected enough to sleep there. It was a summer heat trap, with no ventilation except from the crack in the nailed-shut window, yet the first frosts in fall would seep through the siding like short-tailed shrews.

During our first two years the loft stayed closed, dark, scary. But when the water ran hot, the light shone, the heat radiated and the brick tent encased a hearth again, it was time to designate the loft as a space for creation.

As long as I can remember, I have played at art, dabbled at craft. My grandmother taught me to knit when I was small, and I sewed most of my clothes at school. I learned sculpture and tried to paint. For a while I did pots, but something wasn't right: the mess, the wet, the dependence on kiln and glaze. Only the mesmerizing circles of the wheel entranced me. And so here I turned to wool, to turning fleece into wool, to twisting and plying my need for craft with my love of animals and from them spinning a life.

I had a neighbour who spun. I followed her home from Alderney one day and boldly turned in her lane. She got out of her car, gave me a quizzical look, and I told her my business, asked her to help me, begged for the knowledge to spin. Malka gave me my start right then and there, invited me into her home, her studio, and slowly showed me the wool, the wheel, the magic of thread. She is a meticulous person, and her skeins are perfect. She is an artist, and her concepts are clear. Together we learned the secrets of my sheep (for she has none), the qualities of those first Hamp crosses with their bulky dense wool, and I made my first continuous thread, my first skein, my first pair of socks for my beloved.

The socks didn't happen quickly. I needed equipment and patience and time. I suffered discouragement, despair and rage. At first I tried a drop spindle, an aptly named tool. A simple shaft attached to a whorl, it can be made from a stone and a stick, or a potato pierced with a pencil, or it can be lathed from fine wood. Flicking the whorl sets the shaft spinning and sends the twist up into the fleece, which grows on itself as the spindle gently falls lower and lower. But as the yarn breaks in inexperienced hands, the spindle drops all at once, and the more it dropped the more discouraged I got, and the more it broke. If I could manage to spin a full length of yarn from hands to floor, I would stop and wind the results on the shaft and begin again. But beginning was perilous, so I stood on a chair to increase the length before I was forced to stop and wrap up the strand. It took forever to fill the shaft and the result was grim. It looked nothing like wool in a thread; it was lumpy and uneven, a thin spiderweb filament culminating in a blob of fleece, now thick, now thin, connected by the sheer force of the wool itself, an imbricated fibre, elastic and gregarious, sticking together with microscopic barbs that extended like paper dolls holding endless hands in a row.

I bought a spinning wheel. No more chair standing, or winding, or stopping. The bobbin fills by itself through a mechanical combination of cords or brakes, and the wheel is powered by foot. Both hands are free to feed the fleece, to control the twist, to guide the yarn onto the spool. It looked so easy when Malka spun. Her foot a soft rhythm, her hands relaxed, the fleece feathers in her lap, waiting their turn to fly.

But the wheel lost its pace at my touch; it balked and bumped and turned in reverse. It travelled the floor, trying to flee my heavy foot until I wedged it in place. I abandoned the fleece and retired my hands for the moment to focus just on my foot, gently down and up, down and up, loosening the tension, working with the wheel and establishing a rhythm. So deceptively simple to turn the wheel at a steady pace, so discouragingly difficult.

I would just find my speed, make peace with the wheel, feel ready to add the wool and begin to spin, when suddenly it would stop revolving or reverse. I felt all the frustration of Jason's quest, wondering how I could accomplish the labours necessary for attaining my golden fleece. The wheel was my wild bull, the raw fibres my dragon's teeth, but my desire to succeed finally got me past the dragon (perhaps Malka spelled it to sleep) and the circle whirled, finally; it drew in my fleece and wound my thread on the bobbin.

Miles and miles of locks lay waiting to be formed into yarn, as they grew on the backs of my flock.

BEFORE WE TACKLED the loft, we filled wool sacks in the barn at shearing and brought baskets of luminous fleece with its rich raw smell, thick with lanolin, into the house. There was too much to knit, too little time. I bought a loom and learned to weave. It was an instrument I could play like a keyboard to create full concertos of twills and tweeds, solos of diamond and cross. I used my full reach to throw the shuttle, to catch through the web, a cloth growing under my eyes as I worked. Such comfort in climbing onto the bench, settling up to the beam, positioning my feet on the treadles, working the spaces with my toes, arching my arms for the throw. A settled position, not easily vacated in those days before mobile phones. There were times it was difficult to climb out, entranced as I was by the rhythm, the click of the lams, the scrutch of the reed, the ratchet clicking cloth onto the roller.

At first I had my loom in the kitchen, my wheel by the fire. But the fruit of that loom too often worked its way into the pots on the stove; wool turned up in the stew. And one day, in a fit of frustration with pastry that refused to roll, I went to throw a fistful on the floor and missed. Heddles and reeds, treadles and pawls covered in lard and flour. It was time the loom had a room of its own: the loft.

We shifted the stairs from west to east, filled the north wall with glass, set two dormers on each side and gave them gothic windows crafted by a near-gothic glazier. We argued with our carpenter, coddled him and cajoled him into preserving rather than levelling. From our own bush we harvested fat cedars, and by way of an ancient man with a shingle mill, we roofed our loft with our own wood. Our mason matched the brick with pilfer from a local ruin and built a nineteenth-century chimney pot around the centre flue for the wood stove below.

The low walls were plastered, as were the wide sloping ceilings and angular dormers. And though he cursed the angles, the pargeter found time to help me dress the loom, to grip bundles of taut woolen threads in his dusty hands as I wound them evenly round the beam for a warp. I worked my wool all over the farm while the loft progressed that summer. I harvested dye-plants in the meadow, spun under the trees, wove sawdust into my kitchen fabric. Endless days of creativity followed by painting and varnishing. Smells of boiling greens for dyeing mixed with the scent of freshly cut pine, of plaster, latex, lanolin and turps.

YEARS LATER the smells have changed. There's the wool still, and recently the pungency of a new coat of paint. Fresh pine in the new railing, and the musts and moulds from aging books gathered second-hand for shelves that grow like spiderwebs along the walls. The sounds of shuttles and spindles, clacking of treadles and whirring of wheels have submitted to clatter of keyboard and ruffling of paper. The loom has crept to a corner, and the wheels surround a guest bed. But I do use them still between chapters, and I write my life in spinning, plying, webbing. I write sweaters and shawls from my sheep and scarves from my dogs with the same hands that weave words in the bookish end of the loft.

I climb stairs covered in catalogne, rag carpet created from old curtains and sheets from my youth. And as I rise up above the house, away from the chores and the others, I look out to the trees, the sky, the endless fields and fencerows. The sun on my right in the morning, on my left late in the day, clouds to the north, the grey of November, the snows of winter and the trapped heat in July. It's often too hot or too cold, too bright or too dark, but this loft of my design, roofed from my bush and floored from my loom is my upper region, my air, my sky. It is as close as I get to the heavens.

✦ *FIRST BORN* ✦

≈ BABIES HAD NEVER BEEN PART of the plan—
at least not our babies. Fur and feathers, and tightly
curled wool intrigued me. Animals who grew to maturity in short months, who went on their way, who
walked at birth.

I became accomplished as a midwife to my flock. I
learned to disentangle twins locked in a fatal embrace,
turn breeches, retract tails and find hind hocks. I put
back prolapses and treated mastitis; I urged weak lambs
to suck.

A young chick, curious about the water pail, tipped
over the edge and lay floating one day, eyes open and
staring, body slack. I scooped him out, felt no pulse, but
breathed into his body, pumped his wings in some slap-
stick Holger Nielsen, dried him with the hair dryer, and
he came alive. Lazarus. I seemed to have a knack.

First Born

BEFORE WE CAME here, back in our nomadic days of youth hostels and backpacks, when so many of us seemed to be on the road, we met an American who'd fled his homeland and its military draft. I don't know if we ever really knew who he was or where he was going, but one night in a faraway place, we shared his wisdom, perhaps gave ours. He believed that the only things that couldn't be taken away from us were what we had in our heads and our hands. Knowledge and skill. And that advice shaped us and helped to bring us here, where we learned the minute changes of weather that govern our crops, the moment before the timothy heads up, the imminence of labour for a ewe. I learned to spin and weave, to dye with wild plants, to sow and harvest. And Thomas learned to build, with wood and stone, with logs and fence wire. Each project brought new skills and packed new knowledge into our heads.

We took courses at the agricultural and community colleges down the highway. Carpentry and plumbing, apiculture and sheep, meat production and wool, restoration architecture and woodlot management. We took things apart and learned how they worked. We attempted to put them back together. We watched our neighbours, rode their seed drills, drove their tractors, packed their hay, killed their chickens (well, only once did I do that, but I know I can). We watched calves being born, wrenched out of their mothers with block and tackle. We fed them milk from galvanized calf pails furnished with wide rubber nipples. We helped castrate piglets. Thomas witnessed the butchering of a pig and turned the neighbour's stomach when he rummaged in the hot entrails, searching for an appendix, ever eager over anatomy. Our hands grew calloused and our minds overflowed with information. We trialed and erred and eventually came to understand many different things crucial to life in the country, to life itself, to recognition of our place here.

After five years on the farm, I was just beginning to feel I understood, had mastered some basics, could survive. There was no place for children in my plan. No courses to take, no degrees to be done in parenting.

Then on a night in February, during one of those wintery winters when the snow circles the county like Orion's belt, Thomas got a call. A patient at a farm nearby was in labour. Her husband was blowing the snow from the lane, getting ready to head to the hospital. As Thomas dressed to go, another call came. There wouldn't be time, could he go to the farm? It was two in the morning, pitch dark but for the blizzard, and I nuzzled the pillow while he moved about. "Come with me," he said. "I might need help."

We got in the truck, busted through the snow in our lane and headed east, then north. The drifts made dunes on the road, hillocks from one side, fingering deeper and deeper over the iced gravel, but we bounded through at speed. Thomas is a madman in a storm, can drive through anything. The laneway was clear when we arrived, and we made our way into the house, the only one lit on the line.

I remember daffodils, armfuls of them, brought from Holland by a relative who came to help the family. How could that be? But I remember them, smell them still. The scent hit me at the door, that pungent yellow elixir of spring cutting through the harsh crisp night. And then somehow we were up the stairs, in the bedroom, at the most beautiful scene in the world. Mother and newborn, already come, beaming and perfect and calm. Propped on pillows, the babe wrapped in a blanket on her chest, the mother and her child were still attached by the cord neatly tied twice with clean string. The father, a dairy farmer, was acquainted with birth, knowledgable and strong, delighted with himself and his loved ones.

Thomas cut the cord, separated the two and put the baby in my arms while he checked her mother. The baby in my arms. I was not a holder of babies. This tiny life, only minutes old, in my arms. Her calm warmth, her beautiful skin, her searching eyes. Born at home in her parents' bed. In my arms until her mother was ready to take her, to put her to the breast, to dissolve into the love affair of the nursing couple.

NOT LONG AFTER, I was pregnant. Awaiting my own February birthing, my own beautiful scene. My fear of this change in my life was stiff and persistent, and I laboured throughout the pregnancy to ward it off. I planted daffodils by the dozens, hoping they would cheer me in my postpartum depression in the spring. I put my ram in early, to give me lambs before my baby. I swam through the summer and ran through the fall, and as soon as the snow came, I skied, staying fit, training for the marathon to come, trying to preserve some part of the body I knew so well.

I grew awkward in my chores, lumbered over gates with pails of water. My balance askew, I got knocked down by the ram. I wore coveralls with the buttons undone through the middle; I bent with care. I picked out the stitches in my barncoat zipper, added a triangle of fabric so the coat would fit over my belly, sewed the zipper in place. When lambing began, I felt each of the ewes' contractions, breathed with each push, wondered how on earth my baby would come without small hoofs to pull on, small legs to grasp. And when the time came for docking the lambs' tails and tagging their ears, I stood holding each animal while Thomas performed the surgery, tears pouring down my face with the pain of it all, and determined never to circumcise a son.

In the house my wheel whirred with the sound of spinning lambswool, which I knit into bootees and sweaters and shawls. Tiny clothes from our farmstuffs, all ready and waiting. Bags woven for diapers, blankets shaped on the loom. Dark greens and deep browns, natural greys and pure whites. Not a pink or a blue to be seen. Deep colours, for the depth of my commitment, the well of my hope.

AND SHE FILLED them all, my beautiful daughter. So pink and round and perfect at birth. Too big already for some of the clothes I'd made. She filled our arms, our lives, our home. This country baby, homegrown baby, created without skill or knowledge, who came with love of her own. And the daffodils bloomed for themselves that spring, for there was no depression.

⊶ *SHEARING* ⊷

THE WINTERS IN GREY COUNTY beg for
heavy wool. Snow drifts right over the fence tops, piling
pompoms on the posts when the wind is down. Gates disappear under crisp white hills. Just getting to the barn can
be a chore, with fresh powder thigh deep. Only snowshoes keep me aloft. But except during the worst blizzards, I feed the animals outside.

I take my baby daughter with me. Mobile and toddling by her first winter, she heads out to the barn
encased in her snowsuit, a complicated braid of knitted
cables in grey handspun. Wonderfully warm, it allows
her to move freely, where nylon or Gor-Tex or whatever would not. She stands among the ewes, or sits in
their midst on the snow, and they mill around her
sniffing, recognizing, protecting. She is a part of their
lives, and they of hers.

There is a courtyard by the barn, a sort of sheep

esplanade. Stone walls cut deep into the bank-barn on the north and also mark the eastern edge. The sheep have access to the stable on the other side, but throughout winter they choose to be out. To dot themselves inside the stone walls. Small white humps in a bleached land. Flakes of snow on fleece on snow.

Before feeding them, I pick my daughter up, a fresh bundle of giggling wool, and place her in the playpen made from hay bales or hurdles or whatever's handy. Keep her safe and happy and warm near the lambs, if there are any yet, the chickens if there aren't. I toss sheaves of hay from the mow out to the courtyard, where they punctuate the white with green wind-scattered dots as individual leaves escape the bale. Late harvested timothy sticks like velcro to wool, so each year I hope the grass was cut and baled before it headed up. If I try to pull the timothy heads out of the fleece, a million seeds scurry deep within it for survival. To protect the fleece from chaff, I use square wooden feeders that prevent the sheep from climbing right into the hay and garlanding themselves like Florizel in *The Winter's Tale*. Small bites will dangle from mutton chops, though, and the odd ewe will drag her dinner across another's back.

A tangle of protection: I guard the fleece from contamination while the fleece shields the sheep from the elements. The snow is the best indicator of success, for in the worst storms my ewes will lie snug under their thick snowy blankets. Their fleece insulates them completely; not a ray of warmth escapes to melt a flake. With their feet tucked under their bulging bodies, they silently ruminate, growing lambs and wool.

Wool is the guiltless crop. Nothing dies in its harvest. If left on the sheep, the fleece would eventually shed, pull off in patches on brambles and briars. The sheep would go bald in patches, trip over its own tresses. A sick sheep will shear itself. Illness causes a break across the fibre, which loosens it until the wool falls away in hanks. Left to grow too long, the fleece fills with chaff and dirt, parts along the back with rain, weighs the animal down. If a woolly sheep turns turtle, it will die. A sheep stuck on its back is "cast." Lying upended, legs flailing, it is a comical sight, but if unaided, its rumen fills with gas that cannot escape. The cud cannot move. The animal suffocates.

Shorn sheep trade their wool for new freedom, give up the weight of their world. Cool, sleek, clean and trim. But it's always a risk, shearing. First it's important to pick the right day. March can be spring or winter, lion or lamb itself. The risk of inclemency. In wet weather, wool will soak like a sponge, absorbing a third of its weight in water, and clog the shears. If it's too cold, naked sheep shiver, huddle up together with their backs hunched, their heads down, their backsides bright pink with embarrassment.

My itinerant shearer is small, child-size. Her feet

are as tiny as those of an ancient Chinese aristocrat, though they symbolize anything but leisure. When she glides the long blows, those smooth strokes that guide the shears from the sheep's flank to its head, her body is spread tight against the animal, stretched to the same length. Although her craft is placeless, her method is local, learned from an ambidextrous man who travelled all over the county. With one hand she shears half the beast. Then, with the sheep flashing fleece like a flourish of white-lined cape, she switches hands to complete the other side. It's not the scientific method of the Antipodes, but she wins prizes at the local fairs.

Belly wool and bits go in the bin with the tags or dags, those locks clogged with unmentionables. The rest of the fleece, held together by its own architecture, is thrown high in the air to parachute down to the sorting table, a slatted grid made of wooden strips that rests on portable gates for shearing day and is stored in the mow for the rest of the year. Small bits of second-cut wool, telltale evidence that the shears have shaved twice to cover a mistake in a previous blow, separate and drop through the slats of the open sorting table to the floor. No good for spinning, they sift through. Dross.

The table is large, four feet by eight, but only just holds the freshly shorn sheepcoat stretched like a crucifixion. I circle round it, honouring, pulling off daggy hind bits, hairy leg tops, matted neck wool, and back-chaff. Always I stretch a lock between my hands and tug. If rarely it breaks, I discard it. Not a spinning fleece. If sound and lustrous, with good crimp—regular shiny waves throughout the fibre—I set it aside. One to send to the mill or to keep and spin at home.

The bellies and bits skirted from the edges go into the dag bag and then the fleece is rolled. Lying right side up on the table, its weathered tips are what I see. But as I turn it inwards, folding the sides up to the centre, one at a time, I reveal its inner secret beauty. Then I roll it tightly like a spring roll, (like a tent, my son will say years later) from tail to tip into a springy sphere. Pure wool close to the bone, the heart. Rolled and sometimes tied with paper twine, the fleece is packed in massive burlap wool bags by hand or the small feet of my jumping child. The cuffed sacking unrolls like a lisle stocking as it fills, and is sewn shut with binder twine when bulging.

FOR MANY YEARS we timed our lambs for winter birthing, when it was too cold to shear, so we missed the bodily changes of the pregnant ewes, hidden as they were under heavy woollen coats. By the time their fleece came off, they had returned to their svelte selves, only their swollen udders revealing their fecundity. The early black-faced crosses gave way to woollier breeds, a finely crimped Corriedale influx for a while, and finally the noble Border Leicester, with its Roman nose and wondrous long wool. To relieve the fleece from the stresses of birth, we planned all our lambing for April and our shearing for March.

Ewes can be shorn before lambing, but they mustn't be upended or jostled in the final stages of pregnancy. If shorn too soon, the ewes' new-growth wool will tempt them away from warm shelter, and they could give birth under crisp moons, their lambs weak with hypothermia, wet birth wool dripping amniotic icicles.

Shearing risks revelations. Like gifts, the sheep are decked in seductive packages, the contents known only when the wrapping is off, like Muslim women out of the chador. The gift can be a wonderful surprise, an expected relief or a disappointment. The ewes are unveiled, but unprotected from the elements or from the ram, who sniffs them like new arrivals in the harem. Unfamiliar, beautiful, pristine, paradoxically mysterious in their exposure.

Auspicious surprises are yearling ewes radiant in first pregnancy, their udders tense, teats shiny, their round bellies pushing against the shears. They had been put with the ram in the hope they might conceive, but they are not strictly required to bear offspring in their adolescence. Older ewes, coming to the end of their breeding careers, emerge bony over the hips but rounded below, carrying lambs under stretched tendons, muscles sagging from years of birthing. They too are revealed in their fertile matriarchy, waddling like the aging mothers they are, bellies bulging, their flock-daughters ranging down in age from nearly a decade to a year.

The wool gives up other secrets as it is spread open like a rug on the sorting table. It chronicles a history of the year, marks fever or illness in a narrowing of the fibre, tells tales of breakouts into burdock or rubbings on a rusty fence. Each fleece thrown, skirted, tested, rolled and packed is as personal as a child's blanket. And one is selected for that future honour.

Now naked, the sheep suddenly have space at what were crowded feeders only hours ago. Each animal is miraculously narrowed by six to eight inches on either side. And they reacquaint with renewed friendliness, snuggle close to stay warm. The saved fleece transfers warmth to sweaters, mitts and scarves for my daughter, socks for my man. The daggy ends fertilize and mulch the garden, and the bellies and bits insulate around a window or over a door.

Spring plants sprout dyestuffs to colour the woolly crop: greens from alfalfa, milkweed, and apple bark carefully peeled from prunings as my young one sleeps on warm afternoons. Summer yellows and oranges, tans and purples from the flowers and berries we gather, filling our baskets in the fields, mother and daughter together. The spun skeins of wool are submerged and swirled around like fish waving their tails in vats of colour. They change hue like chameleons, chased by a little girl on a chair, a wooden spoon in her hands.

By summer the sheep have their coats back—they are two inches deep by July. The sheep don't notice their old wool hanging in coils to dry, magically transformed by a mysterious prism. They can't know the magic of green jewelweed chopped into the pot, releasing orange dye like blood from a wound. Surely they don't recognize themselves as clothing on their keepers the next winter, my daughter now bigger, my son stretching my sweaters, almost ready to be born.

They do know the cycle, though, and rarely resist being flipped on their backsides on the shearing board to be pinked-up each year. They relinquish their wool, shake off immaculate bodies, waltz back to the pen like young women in their backyard bikinis on the first hot day in April. All white and shy, but delighted to shed the fat blankets of cold-weather wear. By the time they lamb they have enough wool for baby rugs. As the dams lie in the straw and ruminate, the lambs will perch on their resting backs like loons.

SHEARING EXPOSES bounty and beauty—except for the year of the lice, when the skin revealed was bitten and raw and fleeces were worn and damaged. Like pediculosis in the fair-haired child, sheep lice are invisible in the fleece. They are discreet and tenacious. There had been suggestions. Clues. The new ram, beautifully groomed when he arrived, began biting at his body before he met the ewes. Loneliness, I thought.

Then a general uneasiness in the flock, some wool loss, some rubbing, some scratching. I considered mineral deficiencies, nutritional problems, wool diseases. I sent away fleece and skin scrapings for analysis. Nothing.

But on shearing day, all became clear. Small patches of skin in distress from the biting, large quantities of fleece worried with the scratching. The crop was in ruin and my flock was infested.

We bought powder made from dried tropical plants, donned gloves and masks. A pen of fresh straw was bedded for the treated. Then, one by one, we powdered each animal, raked their backs, rubbed their legs, patted the dust into their bellies. Doom dust. Doom to the lice and boon to the sheep. The air was as white as the swamp in a fog, but the sheep didn't mind. They loved it. Finally the itch was scratched.

One by one they pranced to the new pen, powdered like ladies-in-waiting for Marie Antoinette. In a court dance they went, regal and noble, their noses high and proud. Their lousy wool gone, their fruitful bellies swaying, their tiny tormentors gagging on minute particles of poison plants. We were all white together. And I felt I knew every aspect of every one of my sheep's bodies intimately. Like a lover—no, more like a mother.

◂ *SHOVEL* ▸

I DON'T RECALL WHO noticed the shape of the shovel. A visitor, not a farmer. Someone who knows antiques perhaps. Knows what city people will pay for the unusual, the rustic, the curious and the absurd. I use it, scrape manure with it, edge its rusty blade into corners, haul its excessive weight up to the wheelbarrow. I could get another. A smaller blade, a plastic handle, a lighter model better suited to my frame.

Who first used my cumbersome square shovel? It came with the place, was tossed in a corner of the barn with the junkyard collection of cattle chains, torn rabbit cages, rusty metal sheeting and the silent memories of a thousand animal ghosts. The barn is different now, cleared of rubble, with new floors, new walls, new pens and the tilt put right.

When we first arrived, the barn "was heading south for the winter," said old Tom McNeil, the spitting, farting, flashing-eyed barn fixer we eventually hired. The pressure of the earth against the foundation, banked up to allow the horses, now tractors, to drive up into the mow, slowly edged the whole structure to a lean, the way a horse will tilt a favourite fence post by continually pushing against it, rubbing its flank on the wood, polishing it to a shine, but setting it off the perfect angle.

Just as someone came up with the idea of building barns on a bank, or of building banks up to a barn, some old farmer devised the method of repair when these banks pressured their barns into a lean. Like parasites who take over the host, a bank unchecked can surpass its symbiotic relationship and kill its partner. It can push the whole barn off its foundations, shake the roof alignment, cause an opening here, a loose board there, and before the animals have had a chance to meet their grandlambs, the barn is all in a heap with the first serious windstorm.

The tilt required attention, but everything else in the barn did too. The old separate cattle stalls were hopeless for gregarious sheep who like to huddle together, the cattle chains were superfluous hanging down on broken frames, and the floor was a treacherous maze of various levels and materials. Until I was pregnant the floor hadn't bothered me; I'd climb over the partitions with full pails of water. But a cumbersome belly made me realize how awkward and dangerous the work was with its many pails, many gates and many nails.

The animals' water froze overnight and each morning I pulled out my crowbar, that heavy beast, and pounded the ice, broke through the top, emptied out pails and started again. More than once it resisted my knocks then gave way all at once, sending showers of shards and drops, debris or worse all over us. A chicken-shit facial some days.

New mother ewes, parched from lactating, greedily drank up all I could give. Pails and pails, gallons and gallons, carried one by one, over the gates, through the pens, around the corner of the warren we'd bought. All while I focused one eye on my toddler. The eye in the back of my head, which mothers develop, but never quite trust.

So after a few years of hauling water and tripping on broken concrete, of mucking out the barn by hand because a tractor couldn't negotiate the pens, we hired Tom McNeil, and he came with his jacks, winches, chains and pulleys. He tore out the foundations on two sides, left no post in the corner: the barn was open to wind and light, staying aloft by some magic of angles. The beams in place, the jacks set up, he started to winch. Inch by inch. The barn groaned. It heaved. It sighed and grumbled. "We got her talkin' now," said Tom, his hand-rolled cigarette in the corner of his mouth. Then he left for the weekend, with our barn floating in air, just a mow with a beam and a chain holding fast.

Overnight, a spring storm took out a tree near the house. Flattened it for good. But the barn stood. Held. The wisdom of the barn fixer setting her strong. On Monday Arthur Erwin, the king of concrete in our area, came to pour cement like ambrosia, spread it like molten gold into solid foundations, walls and floors. And my daughter, now strong on her feet, took it all in, stooped for the stones and drew in the muck and made her mark—two tiny footsteps—on this place she calls home. We rebuilt the foundation around her, to buttress her up and make her feel safe. Her sibling was just quickening when we began. I needed a better barn. Where I could walk without tripping, water without pails, feed without shoving. Spend less time on the chores as my family took more.

WHEN THAT PILE of stone and earth had first been bevelled beneath the mow doors, the original barn was big enough to service a full hundred acres, all the grain, straw and hay the farm would grow, as well as the animals it could pasture. Likely the farmers had a cow or two for milk, a few beef cattle, some pigs, sheep and chickens. The barn was built with timber from the forests and stone from the fields. Stones are legion in this township—it sits on glacial moraine. No matter how many stones you pick, the yearly frost always heaves up more. Stone piles are monumental.

The local hemlock, roughly sawn for barnboard, is

no longer available. My good friend and neighbour Harrow, reluctant to replace such boards with pine, which would only last a hundred years or so, clad his barn in steel. I can't help wondering how that will look in a hundred years. Wood is pleasing in a state of decay.

After the first barn burned in the twenties, the owner retired and sold the farm to the next-door neighbour, who was happy to get it—his rocky land was too marginal to support a family well. No doubt the house stood empty for a while, and the barn may have been vacant too. But not for long. The original farmer couldn't cope with town. It must have felt like the city to him—buggies everywhere, telegraph poles and electric lights going in, hustle and bustle as the trains pulled up, groups of people tripping over each other, noisy drunks on a Saturday night. He couldn't take it. He returned, bought back the corner of the farm, the house, the barn, twenty-three acres. And it was then that the barn burned.

So my barn is not all that old. Although the property was cleared well back in the century before the last, and the earliest house—now in ruins—was made of local logs, the first barn did not survive. Old Mr. Meads, a patient of Thomas's, remembers when it burned. He lives in Murphy's Mill now, but he grew up around the corner from our farm. He had been driving cattle down the concession to the railway in Alderney. A sudden storm, thunder, lightning, and the barn was struck. No doubt the fire-reels came, and the neighbours set up a bucket brigade, but only the foundation was saved. The firefighters brag they've never lost a foundation yet. The foundation had been built from the Canadian Shield. Solid as granite.

The smoke from a burning barn carries for miles. Clouds of flames burst through the boards as old hay and straw catch. Buckets of water, or hoses from pumpers filled at nearby streams only wet down the other outbuildings, the house, the nearby wooden fences. A barn fire rarely gets put out. It rages like Hera in a temper, sacrificing heifers, then smoulders in its rocky enclosure, cowed by great hot stones that are impervious to flame and testament to the cold that brought them here.

The township arrives, bringing pies, casseroles, fresh bread and eggs. Farmers take cattle home with them, milk them in their own barns, tether horses in their sheds, pile pigs into their pens for sleepovers. The sheep are on pasture, safely grazing, their wool inflammable, their winter shelter gone but not yet mourned. Dogs sniff and worry and burn their paws in the rubble. They dig and uncover, expose the losses, find the bones.

At one time, there would have been a bee to rebuild. We only see barn raisings now when a local Mennonite barn burns. At the last one, the children were sent from school to watch the raising—it's that rare. But in the twenties, bees were common. In the days before the tin men and the Quonset hut, all the farms were smaller, had more men, more hands, more immediate skills.

Having only a quarter of a farm now, the farmer had no use for a large barn. He couldn't grow enough hay or grain on this land to fill the mows, or sustain a full quota of stock. But he had to rebuild something. Using two sides of the stone foundation and old timber already notched from some derelict barn, he sunk in posts to hold up the south and east sides, laid new mud-sills, created a skeleton, mortised and tenoned. He had help with the frame.

A neighbour up the road had a portable sawmill that ran off the tractor and cut hemlocks from the bush for siding. There was a shingle mill in Alderney where the farmer could take cedar logs from the swamp for the roof. Nails came by the pound then and were square cut and heavy. The preparations were legion and long, but the process reacquainted him with his land and reassured him of his mission. He belonged on this place. His forefathers built the first house, the first barn. He would replace what was lost.

On the day of a raising, folks would arrive early. The men at the barnyard, the women at the house and yard. Boys would set up tables and unload benches and chairs from the wagons. Dogs would bark. Babies would sleep under nets beneath maples or nurse in the upstairs rooms. Cats would emerge from their hiding spots, hunker down at a distance and watch. Milk came in cans fresh from the cold house, produce came from the gardens, berries directly from the bushes, bread from twenty ovens. Woodstoves in surrounding kitchens would roast meat, making the women sweat into their bib aprons, their hair escaping from pins and flattened against red faces. Women with names like Bertha and Beulah, Clover and Cavelle. Rubys and Olives and Ferns, their last names carried on by brothers. Little girls would draw out the cloths, set the tables, place the forks, the knives, the cups. Cauldrons of water would be set to boil for tea, hams sliced, eggs hard-cooked, peeled and devilled.

Preserved herbal vinegars, pickles, relishes. Salt, pepper, sugar. And pies. The pies would be competitive—practice pieces for the fall fair. Rhubarb, raspberry, apple and cherry, elderberry from last year's canning—the elderberries not yet ripe in midsummer— perhaps the odd peach from someone who had been down-country and was showing off. The elevation won't tolerate peaches here. They die off in frosts.

Days of preparation for this feast. Two feasts, for after the noon dinner the men and bigger boys would be back at the barn, would work until supper, would need to eat again before going back to their own chores, their own barns. So the women would scurry and sweat and worry and fuss and work as hard as they did then. The food had to be beautiful, had to be nourishing, and it was.

Tom McNeil's father was the barn wizard before him, and he would lead the team, organize the men into what they did best. The sure-footers to the roof, the land-lovers to the foundation. The reckless in tandem with those with a good sense of self-preservation. The doctor on standby, ready to deal with concussion, splinter and gash. No one wore protective equipment. And, as the pies were contested in the house, skill and speed were winning elements at the barn. Who could lay more shingles? Who could carry more boards, hammer more nails, set in the best windows?

The men would bring their own tools. Some in leather aprons. Hammers hooked to overalls. Ladders and squares, levels and plumb lines, cloth tapes in leather cases, saws, planes and chisels. A neighbour needed a barn. Lightning strikes. It might happen to you someday.

It might have been Aaron Wilson who brought the shovel. He mixed cement, poured the sidewalks in Alderney. The shovel's blade can hold a heavy dollop of muck and the shaft has the ghost of concrete in its cracks. But the tool must predate him too, that split wooden handle, carefully steamed to bend, chosen from the lathe for its strength and resilience both. Whoever brought it, forgot it. Or left it as a talisman, like the branch of evergreen on the ridge, spirit of safety for those who must not fall.

⤙ ZOË ⤚

⟿ THE STABLE FLOOR is indelibly marked, not only with the named and dated sneakered footprints of my toddling daughter, but with a trail of errant paw prints angling across one corner, hidden all year by bedding and sheep. Each summer, on the day the barn is cleaned out and the manure is spread on the hayfield, the paw prints resurface. They are the lasting marks of a sappy dog who started and ended her days here.

Zoë was born right in the middle of the back kitchen early in our first spring, before the renovations, when the floorboards were broken and the wind howled through. Her mother was a city mongrel, probably a mix of hound and shepherd, though Thomas's grandmother said she was "a bit big for a Heinz."

I'd never had a dog before, though I'd longed and begged for one, even brought puppies home when I was a child, trying to break down my parents' resolve. Zoë's mother, Jessie, just a stray pup, was injured at the side of a city road. A vet wrapped her broken leg to her body until it healed, and found her a home with us before we came here. She began a three-legged race (the fractured leg never touched the ground at speed) that lasted for fourteen years.

Zoë's father was a Grey County local, a daily visitor who had a reputation for being the best groundhogger in the township. His title was undisputed by any of the neighbours. A crucial task, dispatching groundhogs is a prized skill because groundhog holes are killers. A cow can break a leg if it drops in a hole. A farmer can fall from his tractor and die if a wheel goes in. When they aren't in their burrows, groundhogs spend most of the daylight hours eating vegetation that has been planted for other uses. Pasture, hay and gardens are all at risk from the woodchuck, *Marmota monax*. So Zoë's sire was legendary. His owner, who lives across the way, was born in this house years ago in one of the upstairs rooms, so it seemed appropriate for the dog to colonize the farm with his pups. Pure white, he had upstanding perky ears and a curly tail, which made a rather odd mix in the offspring. Some had floppy hound ears, others had ears that stuck right up, but Zoë's were that fetching combination that begin by sitting up straight, but turn over at the edges, limp-eared, as if the starch ran out at the laundry.

As a newborn she was almost totally black, but over

the months her markings changed. The dark hair remained over her head and back, but formed a wide symmetrical band around her face, detailed with tan. Her legs and belly turned beige and she grew a white ruff. The older she got, the more her white father surfaced in her fur, eventually making her Snowy Zoë and Snowface.

She was the runt of six pups, the last born, and she retained a bit of the underdog in her demeanour. Her effective bark did little to ward off strangers, for as soon as anyone approached her she'd turn turtle and submit. Zoë shadowed her mother sideways through fences, trailed behind her over the hills, and lost all their games of bite-throat, throwing herself down on her back, her mother's teeth pointed at her neck. Never could she get enough attention.

At thirty-five pounds, she made a rather cumbersome lapdog, but she was determined to live on the couch, snuggle up and settle into quiet adoration. She turned into a rag doll then. We would gently clutch the tendon in the crook of her front leg to make the relaxed paw rise and fall in a wave. She would be on her back, her chin high in pleasure, her eyes half closed.

Zoë loved to sing. When she was on her back, on my lap, I'd rub her chest and hit a note, and she'd start in on an uninhibited aria. Tremulous, melodic, Zoë's operatic numbers far surpassed the baying of hounds at moons. My guess is she'd have loved the costumes of formal performance as well. But Zoë was a farm dog.

She inherited her father's skill at groundhogging. Her mother was a natural killer as well, but Zoë was a pro, an Artemis, eagle-eyed and fast. Her aim was perfect and her method, which was to attack and shake, broke the groundhog's neck in an instant. Sweet singer, she turned vicious when a woodchuck showed its yellow teeth.

Groundhog bodies would lie in state for a few days, depending on the heat, before Zoë would drag them home for a final ripening on the lawn. When they were really rank, she would alternately chew away on them and roll in them, spreading the scent of rotting flesh all along her coat before begging for an evening lap-sit. She got to sleep outside in the summers.

It seemed incongruous to breed Zoë, a perpetual pup, so we took her into Murphy's Mill to be spayed after her first groundhogging season. It was autumn, the vermin were gone to ground for the winter, and she'd begun to smell more like a dog than a charnel house. She would be able to convalesce inside.

Because Zoë had a hidden infection, something went wrong during the anaesthetic. She lost vital signs, went into cardiac arrest, turned flat. The vet jumped all over her, administered life-saving drugs, did CPR, bagged her, got her breathing again. Whatever was wrong was beyond his scope and equipment. Guelph, he said. We had to rush her to the animal hospital at the agricultural college. It was the only way to save her.

Thomas drove the pickup. Zoë lay unconscious on my lap in the passenger seat, her reflexes too shallow now for even a wave. I cradled her in one arm and held up the IV bottle with my other. An hour's drive down the highway, ambulance speed, taking our dying dog to the best veterinary care in the country. Thomas, used to tending emergencies along the same route on code 4 trips to the hospital, was reduced to relative and driver.

We left her at the college in the care of the vets. They called us in the middle of the night and I heard Thomas try, through the fog of sleep, to make sense of what they were saying, try to translate dog-owner talk into medical language so he could really understand. "You mean she has peritonitis?" he asked and pressed for details. It was touch and go. She was infected, was in grave condition. They had removed what damaged tissue they could, cleaned up the rest, put her on drugs and were waiting for improvement. She was stable.

Such a sad face she had when we arrived to take her home. Hound eyes turned down, great pools of liquid beseechment. We'd abandoned her, she was broken and rent, but we were back. She rode home on my lap, gazing up at me with longing, with promise, with submissive adoration. A quiet dog for the moment, the hunter asleep inside.

It wasn't long before her spark returned and she got back outside, firing herself through the fences on tilt. She ran the ski routes all winter chasing rabbits and

foxes, flushing birds out of the bush. And after running the trails she'd come inside, chew the ice from her
paws and loll on her back, waving, singing, dreaming
and running on the spot.

We had a rabbit in the house by then. Thlayli, an
angora with a furry head. I'd won him in a hand-
spinning competition. His hair was long, blueish-grey
and fine, and he'd sit on my lap to be combed and
plucked. When he wasn't in his cage in the front hall,
he had the run of the house, and Zoë tolerated him the
way she did everything else.

In the summer, Thlayli lived outside. I made a
wooden house for him, which I put inside a moveable
wire-mesh enclosure. Every few days I moved it to a
new place on the lawn so he could graze. Of course
he'd inevitably get out of his enclosure by burrowing
under it, or by hopping around during the move. He
was tame and always returned to his hutch. His first
summer passed without incident, Zoë nosing him
when he escaped.

During his second spring, Thlayli was shifted once
again to his outside home. But his first free hop along
the grass was his last. Zoë must have seen a moving blur,
and she pounced. She grabbed, shook and broke his
neck. Just like that. A pile of dead angora lay limp on
the lawn.

It was clear that Zoë knew what she'd done.
Contrition is evident in a dog. The eyes, both avoiding

connection and begging forgiveness. The tail dragging, the ears off their semi-perk. Zoë never killed the wrong thing again. The chickens were safe; the cats untouched. For the rest of her life she killed ground-hogs until they all but disappeared from the farm, but nothing else.

She'd been a digger through the years. There was a spot by the house, under the lilacs, that she'd hollowed out on the hottest days each summer, trying to find a cool den. We gave up trying to stop her. If caught in the act she just showed her belly and exposed her neck. Old age crept up too soon, seven years at a time, and Zoë finally sang her last song. Thomas dug down into the spot under the lilacs she was always trying to reach, deep enough so she'd be cool forever. As I mourned, he laid her to rest just a few feet away from where she was born. She's there by the house, but her footprints still sprint through the barn each summer, and her memory lives in the generations of groundhogs whose ancestors moved to safer terrain.

⊰ *DARK DAYS* ⊱

⫷ THE BARN WAS TRANSFORMED by the renovation Zoë had witnessed. The floor was smooth and flat but for the paw- and footprints; the walls were straight. We installed heated water bowls in the chicken coop, and on both sides of the stable floor to provide access to the greatest number of pens. The main beam was replaced, the mud-sills renewed.

Almost nothing was built in, just the centre posts and troughs. The space was immense, wide open and clean. Tobacco tins, sunk in the floor when the cement was being poured, left post holes when dry for arranging our pens. We drew up plans at the kitchen table, Thomas and I, with cement-king Arthur's help. Formations for feeding, for lambing, for mothering up. Sick pens and ram pens and pens for fattening late lambs. Pens for yearlings and new stock and creep-feeding—where lambs can squeeze through a small opening for feed, their greedy but frustrated mothers left behind. All possible arrangements with portable housing. The stable stanchions and mangers now mutable gates and hurdles, feeders and pens.

THE WINTER WE SPENT before the renovation was worse than the state of the barn. The ram had got out the previous summer, had bred some of the ewes before the prime time. This increased my workload because I had to feed the imminent ewes differently from those more recently bred. It all might have worked if I'd stayed to conduct the proceedings. But I got sick. Really sick. Hospital sick. Out of town sick. A terrible infection. And there was nothing I could do but lie in bed, fight for my health and fuss for my family, my farm, my still-nursing daughter, my unborn lambs.

I was filled with drugs, and I thinned and weakened and despaired more each day. My milk almost went, but I would not force a weaning on my daughter. It was for her to choose when to stop.

The hospital was in the city, two hours away. Thomas, so busy at work, on call so much, so many needing him, did everything. He brought me the baby, looked after the barn, tended his patients and worried like crazy, his knowledge a curse. And one full-moonlit night, one of the ewes wandered out into the light and gave birth in front of the barn. Triplets. Dropped in the snow during a frostbitten night, left to freeze in their sacs with no one to help.

It went on all winter, day after day, recovery and relapse, trips down the road to the hospital. Once, Thomas was on call—the emerg full of carnage and crises—and had to see me himself. I needed more care, but the ambulance was taken by a patient of his, and there was no room for me. So I waited until the neighbouring town sent theirs, which was more primitive than ours and without trained staff. The attendants did not know my illness, couldn't have helped if they did. They asked me directions to the city, to the health centre, to an all-night gas station along the way. Panic set in and added to my pain. How did Thomas manage to care for others—his duty clear and unflinching—while I was so ill?

We were still newcomers (as we always will be) and we kept to ourselves. We were given distance perhaps, and we took it too. We didn't ask for help; we didn't make it known that we couldn't manage. But help came along—food at the door, childcare and cleaning, barn work too—until my surgery in March brought a slow return to health. From being vibrant and strong, I turned weak and inept, hardly able to care for any of my charges or do any of the chores or contribute to the life we were making. Dark days, dependent days. The whole point of being here was to cope on our own, to do it ourselves, to turn knowledge and skill into self-reliance and autonomy.

THOUGH THE SUN was increasing, that spring held the hardest days, the longest nights, when I looked at the future and saw only clouds. I lay on the couch, unable to muster the strength to go out. My daughter was being cared for by others. I was caught in some underworld, punished perhaps for unknowingly tasting a seed I'd never noticed. Bitter suffering after sweet fruit.

But slowly the weight went back on, the muscles recovered. The spring daffodils—unnecessary after my daughter's birth—did their job. The second crop of lambs, whose mothers eschewed the ram's early caprice, arrived strong in April, and I tended them gently—not without incident, though, as the weather grew cruel and again my barn visits were fewer. There were times when the house was a playpen of bellowing young, all dressed in diapers, all needing care. Sick lambs by the fire, tails emerging from holes in their disposables, stroked and loved by my child, herself still swathed in cloth. And the ache of the deaths, which inevitably occurred, tore at my heart for my neglect.

So we needed the barn. Needed changes and care. Needed simplicity of design and ease of access. Needed to sweep out the ghosts of that horrible year where everything went wrong and fell to chaos. We had no thoughts of quitting, despite all the failure. We forged ahead with new plans. We carried on.

The hope May brought sifted gently through our days, carried us aloft on soft winds. Early planting, careful planning, thinking ahead. And as life all around us settled, the future came clear as I conceived once again.

We spent a glorious summer rebuilding the barn, redoing the nursery and growing our crops. Putting disaster behind us and looking beyond and also back to the dream that brought us here. Staying strong in our need to succeed and our love of the land and each other. But wellness eluded me once winter came; the baby refused to stay still. He rolled and thundered in turmoil inside, trying to emerge ahead of his time. More truck trips and ambulances, rides to the city. Thomas again on call at a delicate moment—an erstwhile brogue-brained colleague refusing to cover the emergency ward—and I found myself alone once more in an ambulance, not knowing if my baby would be born or would live, his father left behind to care for others.

But we stayed symbiotic, my baby and I, and drugs kept him inside and protected from light. Once home, I was back on the couch, my daughter shipped out, my belly threatening to heave and contract whenever I walked to the barn. Stuck once again, unable to work, dependent on others for help. Until my baby was born, all in a flash, his father lovingly guiding him out in the rush. Perfect and tiny and looking like me, though early and slightly underdone. Caught and held first in his father's arms. Like a kitten, his eyes not quite open, his hands folded up, his attitude lazy and soft. I was instantly better, motherlove strong, and my chores seemed possible, my work looked clear.

Everything flourished in the house and the barn. The setbacks seemed insignificant after all the stress. And the months and the seasons settled into a pattern, changing only with growth and language and skills in my children, my farm children, who knew nothing but this place as home, who took to the animals and chores and rhythms of the day as they did to breathing the air of the country around them.

⊰ *SNAKE* ⊱

IN THE YARD, THERE IS A HUMP in the turf, a ridge about half the length of a country laneway, which remembers a time before grass. Previous farmers ploughed in front of the house, grew those dour mangels whose discarded beety corpses were still rotting when we arrived. We seeded our permanent pasture with a mixture of grasses and clover, filling in the furrows and greening the area, but the ridge remains. A reminder that this is not really a lawn, a playground, a croquet pitch, but a reclaimed field.

Before it was a field, it was a forest, or perhaps a small meadow surrounded by forest. What feet walked here before we came? Feet that trod four at a time or that were shod in doeskin. Feet that remain, reflected in their descendants, or remembered only at a remove, on reservations.

What footprints lie in the soil, what tales in the weeds? It is said that burdock and thistle seeds will live for hundreds of years, will lie dormant until the soil is disturbed, until somebody digs, somebody ploughs, somebody plants. Then the weeds come out of the dark. Like Persephone they find the light and have their short season in the sun, send up their flowers, more purple than pomegranate—the colour of kings— to ripen, dry and form snagging seeds, waiting for something unsuspecting to cling to. On four feet or two, they are transported.

The earth knows these stories and a thousand more. Subterranean cities shelter cultures older than Hades's underworld, cultures where even feet are superfluous. Under the hump in the turf, under the ridge, lives a colony of creatures that may have been there before the glaciers reshaped the landscape, scraped the rocks and ground them up and left behind the gravel pits and stone deposits and bits of fossil and shale that underlie the soil.

It takes a sunny March day to bring these squigglers to ground. One of those days when the sap runs. When it's cold at night and there's frost under a clear sky, but sun on the snow at dawn, casting long silver and blue shadows that turn to gold before dusk. These are days when the snow sublimates, misses that melting step and goes directly from solid to vapour, disappearing before your eyes to reveal patches of winter grass, that dead, brown cover thatched over the earth, dormant, dank, but hopeful. Mindful of its possibilities, its past, its future. Such patches will dry out with a few of these days, surrounded still by corn snow, pitted honeycombed white ice. And the snakes will pass from underworld to over.

These are days when melting snow reveals lost treasure. Finding days. In the city, coins and ribbons, buttons and marbles, mittens and toques appear. But in the country, the treasure is more fundamental. We found the snakes one year by accident, by surprise. The children and I were on an expedition. The snakes were not lost, not mislaid. We are the interlopers; this is snakes' country.

They are garter snakes, fondly called gardener snakes around here. Or gardner 'nakes on the tongue of my daughter, the ear of my pre-lingual son. We found perhaps a hundred of them, babies, all bunched together like spaghetti in a pot, swirling and wriggling, arcing over one another like porpoises diving, like frogs leaping, like kittens nursing. A living mass of cold-blooded reptiles undeterred by the thinning ozone, warming their bitter blood in the light of day, in the spring of time.

As long as the sun shines, the snakes stay. When it withdraws, they descend out of sight, not on ladders, but by slithering down like fast rain on a windowpane, one fat drop at a time. The earth looks like Swiss cheese. But only if you get close; only if you know where to look. And the season is short before the snake commune disperses: it can be missed.

As spring progresses and the grass greens and grows, the snakes separate, leave home, stake out their own ground. Garter snakes travel alone. Svelte bachelors, they make their own fun. Some even live in the city, cruising backyards and boulevards, making double entendres with forked tongues.

The country snakes, the farm snakes, have their own modes of sophistication. If they can stay off the gravel roads, avoid the fast wheels of passing trucks and tractors, stay out of the mower's way and evade the teeth of the hay baler, country snakes have a good chance of survival. When things get tight, they can always change their skins, discard them on the grass and slide into something more comfortable. Like gossamer sent soaring by a breeze, the shimmering, empty body stocking is too fragile to hold. A fine serpent mould, it defies refilling, and despite its stunning segments, it disappoints. Mere nail clippings.

THERE IS A GARTER SNAKE lying out on the sun-baked stones of the house foundation where I keep the summer hose. A large, thick, powerful snake in new skin. The area around the window well is dug up, exposed. In the fresh dirt hops a toad, oblivious to everything but mud and earth and new scenery. He has his toad thoughts from his toad day. A sudden strike and the toad turns turtle. The snake snaps his huge jaw and bites down hard on the toad's belly. The toad thrashes his legs, screams. The snake gyrates until he is almost vertical, and the toad flails one foreleg, not waving. Then, inexplicably, the toad is free and it lopes off into the dirt. Surely the snake can see him and attack again?

With freshly dug potatoes resting in my gathered-up shirt-tail, I stand open-mouthed, mesmerized, relieved the toad is free, but unable to find a role for myself in this scene, which is as strange as it is Homeric, Biblical, Miltonic.

Unimpressed by the high drama, the snake slithers between the stones of the usually subterranean foundation and disappears. I dump my potatoes on the grass and turn the hose on them, converting the encounter to dailiness, washing away the taste. But from his hiding place, the toad reappears and for some incomprehensible reason jumps back into the window well. Like lightning the snake strikes and clamps his jaws on the toad's back.

I can no longer watch passively. I grab a stick and prod the snake. My need to protect the weak, foster the homely. The toad escapes and the snake goes back into the dark, a guilty underworld he inhabits alone. I place the toad in the impatiens, across the grass from the window well.

Inside, I find a bowl for the wet potatoes, hear my babies begin to stir from their nap, and ache with fierce protection. I try not to think about what snakes eat for dinner. Or toads.

⤛ CROWBAR ⤜

⫇ I GREW UP IN AN OLD HOUSE with a basement full of tools. I spent my summers in a cottage with three woodsheds (one an old ice house), a pumphouse, a garage and two boathouses full of tools. Tools were always around, strewn about the floor of a workspace, carefully arranged on walls, hanging from ceilings, packed in tool boxes. I'd seen everything performed, from spray-painting a car from black to white, to dynamiting a huge rock deemed too close to a cabin, to cutting an outbuilding in two with a handsaw, pulling it apart and building a new middle section.

When I left home my father's parting gift was a paper bag with a hammer, a couple of screwdrivers and a metal tape measure. No books, no cash, no philosophy: just tools. I have them still.

On the farm, tools are not just a necessity. They are monumental. Barn tools, house tools, fencing tools.

Shearing tools, lambing tools, glazing, wiring and plumbing tools. Carpentry I knew about. Hammers, squares, saws. Crosscut and rip, mitre and keyhole, coping and hack. Fasteners I could do: Robertson, Phillips, slot; screws, nuts and bolts; nails: ardox and plain, round and square.

I was familiar with the crowbar. My father had several in different sizes, curved, bent up to a spur at one end, slotted as if to pry loose giant nails, but I don't remember seeing them used. They were around, with the sledges and axes, the big tools with handles, the dangerous ones with sharp edges.

My first crowbar was not really a crowbar at all. It was a wrecking bar, fondly called "Barry's tool" after its bestower, who was one of our first visitors to the farm. He was big enough to tear just about anything down by hand, but he realized I would need a little help. It was blue rather than black, about as long as a raven, curved, beaked at one end, clawed at both. Iron, strong, it could lever out anything from square nails to bedroom walls. And it did. And it does.

More than most tools, the crowbar is a rearranger. Hammers create, saws shape, wire enlightens and pipes irrigate. But the crowbar pries, levers, moves, pushes or destroys. It can be a mean ugly tool with teeth at both ends—tooth and claw—hungry to deconstruct. It was created to destroy. The crowbar is formed from iron over fire. Whether created by ancient god, from

Hephaestus at his forge to Vulcan at his anvil, or recent humanity, this tool is a brute born to maim.

I had thought all crowbars had beaks. Named for their ornithological namesakes, called simply crows originally, they possess bills, not for tearing carrion or plucking lambs' eyes, but for destroying nature's grip or civilization's detritus. Their heads curve like the pate of the bird, their tails notch like the crossed feathers of folded wing-tips. All crowbars assumed that shape in my mind until I found, at a nearby auction, a tall staff of iron, straight, hand-hammered, blunt-topped from the swing of a thousand sledges, wedged to a running point below. High as a corn stalk, heavy as an anvil itself, it was a barn of a crowbar. A farmer's crow.

"A corn planter," said my neighbour, baiting me. "Just stick it in the ground to make a hole, drop in the seed and you're away." And he wasn't all that far wrong. Such straight crowbars were once used to make irrigation holes around saplings. Seed drills and corn planters operate on that ancient principle of making a hole, planting a kernel.

The crowbar came home with me, found a spot in a nook in the feed room, by the door, leaning up against the corner. It can't hang upright on the wall as it has no curve. It looks light there at its jaunty angle, like a marshmallow toasting stick, or a fishing rod, or a beanpole. But each time I reach for it I am surprised at the weight of such a solid piece of iron, and I wonder how the Greek god of fire managed to lift such ore in his lameness.

MY TOWNSHIP is glacial moraine. Good drainage. Groundhog heaven. But with the gravel comes the rock. Billions and billions of rocks. Our best crop. Each year the frost shifts them and raises them like wind on water. Waves of rocks. Usually, just where I want to put a garden, a post, a fence, a tree, is where the rocks will swell and build, collect in an undertow. Fields that fell asleep in the fall under striped loam shag, awake in the spring grey-patterned with stone heaved up from the underworld by angry shades, bleached by snow and sleet, polished by April rains. Defiant, proud, solid, stationary. Or worse, the stones huddle just beneath the surface of the earth, pitting ploughshares, dinging double-discs, havocking harrows. The front-end loader and the back-hoe have replaced the stoneboat, the crowbar, the board and the barrow for removing rocks to centre piles, fencerows, low spots. A lone tree or small grove in the middle of a field is never really on its own in this county. It is moated by stone. Small mammals find their own labyrinths, fear their own Minotaurs.

A century of moving rocks, wrestling them out of the way of horses' hoofs (duly shod with iron), of iron implements, heavy tractors of iron and then steel. Iron and steel: iron and rock. Alloys but never allies. Metal and rock pitted against each other in a battle for the soil. For crops can't grow in stone.

Within the farmyard, in places where tractors can't go, places too narrow for front-end loaders, too soft for heavy horses, the stones do not spare the garden soil but congregate, conglomerate like fireflies over a swamp in July. At Lambsquarters there are few places a shovel will sink without ringing, clanging, jolting your wrists on its handle, the blade starting like a knife through butter, stopping short on Hadrian's Wall. And no matter how often it happens, it is always a disappointment. The earth fighting back, hindering, defying the planter, laughing. Often the tip of the blade will loosen a garden stone, wiggle it to an edge, tilt and wobble it until there is some purchase and the stone rises, brown and dull and way too small to have caused this annoyance. A pup of a stone, without character. I pitch these over the fence and into the field, knowing I probably shouldn't, that they could get caught in machinery, but hoping they are too insignificant to cause more harm. The blade goes back in, slides, then clangs again. The jerk travels up my arms, through my carpal tunnels, inflaming the tendons in my elbows. Another small stone, snug beside the first, to be prised, coddled, entreated to the top. Picked and tossed with disrespect.

An afternoon of this is at best burdensome, slow work. The children bored and grizzling in the sandbox.

The waiting plants wilting, crossing their drying roots with impatience, tapping their leaves, nodding their flower heads, wondering if they will ever find their place in the ground. At worst, I'm left with a broken shovel handle. For inevitably there is a rock that seems like a stone, which nudges from an edge, which seduces with smooth moves, but which is pure rock. It could be the size of a fat hen or a small island. It might outcrop on the other side of the world. Or perhaps it is just stuck. It begs to be levered, then breaks the shovel. Just above the metal, the wood cracks and splits. The rock wins.

The crowbar never breaks. It will get the rock out or it won't, but the rock won't get the crowbar. For large jobs—deep fence posts, foundations, a geological monster in the vegetable garden—the crowbar is the obvious tool. But yearly I am fooled by shallow jobs, and handles break, trowels are bent beyond use, defeated by rocks, while the crowbar leans against the barn wall in the shade, as if watching me.

THERE ARE TIMES I want to use the crowbar for something other than digging out stones. It would make a perfect temporary fence post—strong, pointed, easily hammered into this resistant earth. The chickens might stay in an outdoor run all summer with the crowbar as a corner post. Or how many scarlet runner beans would climb it, solid and reliable in the garden, bashed in and secure? No delphiniums would topple in summer storms if attached to this staff.

But the crowbar is too important for digging and prying to do a locum as an upright. All summer there are cedar posts to replace, to prise out after they've broken off just beneath the surface, wedged as they were half a century ago with stones and rocks from the original hole. There are stone walls to build and rebuild from first clearings. And did this bar in those times walk these hills and move these rocks? Did it pry stones from the meadows, tilt them onto stoneboats or barrows and roll them into cairns like centrepieces on the tables of the fields? Does the crowbar feel the same stone it moved eons ago from the nearby field where I bought it? And will it still be here in the hands of my unsuspecting children's heirs to move rocks from the rock pile to the rock wall and back a hundred years hence?

⤙ *RAIL FENCE* ⤚

🪶 THE PIE-SHAPED FIELD is wedged into a hill
with the point sloping down into a valley. One side,
along the top of the ridge, verges on cedars, and the
upper edge is line fence, boundary with the neighbour
to the north. At the bottom of the hill, which approaches
the forest, the fence is split-rail, made in the century
before last from the cedars cleared from the field. The
rails snake and angle in a rabbit run, zigging around
boulders, zagging through trees. They skew obliquely,
defying geometry, and are stacked a full seven rails high.

An excellent material, cedar. Free for the clearing.
All that's needed is the toil to cut and split, stack and
sweat them into place. Only that. Born in the swamp,
cedars take to water, resist rot and stay strong while the
maple leaves mould around them, as the forest turns
into earth and the earth turns into trees. Eastern White
Cedar is native to the Great Lakes–St. Lawrence

Region, the Acadian forest and the boreal as far north as James Bay. It likes the swamp, which isn't too acid, not too sharp, with limestone tucked neatly below. It will grow over sphagnum bog, but not as well, preferring moist soil to make it tall and fat. It can reach a full eighty feet high and three feet across, but few grow that big. Its roots are shallow, precarious to wind, which will lift up its feet, toss them over, expose spindly underpinnings to the rodents who burrow beneath.

The tree of life, arborvitae, so named because it treated scurvy in Cartier's crew.

Its bark is stringy, soft and fibrous. Perfect for squirrels to feather their nests in spring, for kids to pull like ribbons as they race through the woods in the fall when their father takes them to help with the yearly tending and mending of the fence. Thomas carries his swede saw, his axe and a coil of wire in the wheelbarrow, his fence pliers in his pocket. These are all the tools he needs to tighten the fence for the winter to come.

Snow is the fence's enemy, snow and deadfall and too many feet scrambling over the rails, climbing between posts where the weaknesses lurk, prying off bits and stressing the wood.

Because of the way the fence lies, north and south with the edge of the wood to its west, it is protected, sheltered from frost, guarded from rain. There is no snow load pushing it down, or heaving against it with the force of nature, the sheen of silver. But in a storm the west wind finds the high branches of the sugar maples, hurls them down, pounding the fence, snapping a top rail, injuring a stake, shifting a wire askew. And so the inspection.

Autumn is a time for putting the farm to bed for the winter. We bring the sheep into the fold from their summer pastures, mulch the gardens with blankets of straw, snug the house with storm windows and doors and stack the woodshed to its rafters with fuel. Thomas takes our son and daughter with him to check and strengthen the rail fences when the weather turns and the leaves have abandoned their branches and line the forest floor. Crunching through the mulch like miniature soldiers, their red and blue rubber boots disappearing in the burnt umbers and scarlets and siennas that rise to their knees, the children swoop down for armfuls, which they pitch to a sky now forked with the bare branches of dormancy. No matter that their tosses are only inches above them, their eyes focus far, they see their leaves fly beyond the tallest tree, and they feel sure they've sailed beyond the limits of the sky's roof. And while they play, their father steadily checks each wavering section of the fence, each turn of the stake. These are not posted panels, only precariously staked corners balanced and counterbalanced: tree roots, rocks, boulders and stumps left no choice for the fencer, who could only go around them, never through. The snake slithers with grace through terrain that would never accept the spade.

Each section, half a rod or so, joins up with its neighbour at a right angle (or less, or more) depending on the trees it embraces, and rests its head on the other's tail. Stakes are pounded in on each side of the join with the butt an axe or the head of a maul and then wired. Number nine, still the farmer's friend. A wrap, a twist, a clip. The fence pliers do the job all in a trice, their gripping jaws the perfect size, thin enough to grab in small sections, strong enough to grasp. They have snipping blades all round, opposing angles meeting in a pinch of wire shiny at its break.

The children wear themselves out running back and forth as their father moves at a measured pace from rail to rail, the dog now panting at his side, now herding the kids or rabbits or flushing a grouse. The children's cheeks redden, their hair fills with chaff and they invent horse and saddle trees, witch and wardrobe trees, and stumps that turn into stages for impromptu puppet shows. Before the fence is done, their games are through. They whinge and stamp and want to go home until finally, the fencerow fixed, their father bundles them into the wheelbarrow and pushes them up the hill, through the field and to the house where I make hot chocolate with melting marshmallows on top and listen to the tales of the woods. An opera for three voices.

⊰ *HEN AND EGG* ⊱

WHEN SHE IS JUST ABOUT to lay an egg, a hen lifts herself up slightly from her sit on the nest. Though she doesn't really stand, she lifts herself higher than a dog would sit, hunkered down on its hind legs, or even than a puppy would sit, one leg lagging to the side. A hen assumes more of a crouch. With her head thrust slightly forward, wings at her sides, she pops her tail up, stretches her legs and rises to a squat. A combination of plié and curtsy culminating in an egg.

During the time she spends in the nesting box before she lays an egg, a hen tucks her legs out of sight like a figurine. Each hen, in succession, tends to choose the same spot in the large nesting box for her deposit. If you can't wait for a sitting hen to finish her lay, you can reach under her to gather eggs from the clutch that has amassed by mid-morning—well you can, but sometimes you pay for it with a quick beak to the hand. The hens in my coop are gentle; not one has pecked me, despite my burrowing in under the soft bodies and rolling eggs away. But when I reach under a sitting hen, I'm gathering the eggs laid by her neighbours. She sits in anticipation of laying, not hatching. *Her* egg is yet to come.

Laying hens, battery hens, are selected to produce eggs, not incubate them. But a Bantam hen will sit on anything. It is her vocation to brood. My father-in-law says a Banty would sit on a piece of shit if she thought it would hatch. She does think it will hatch. She's quite sure of it. She will sit for days past the hatching time. Eternal hope of the Banty. These hens are so good they hire out. They hatch pheasants, ducks, anything ovular that they can shelter under their feathery girth.

The protective instinct is linked with broodiness. Interfere with the sitting Banty and you get pecked. Get too close to a Banty rooster and you get attacked. They are small, tough, scrappy individuals, richly coloured and diversely marked. No two barnyard Banties are quite alike—some have feathered legs, some have spurs. They dress like courtesans and biker sluts. But they love their eggs, and if they decide to take a turn at sitting on them, there's not much you can do but wait for the chicks to poke and peak their way through their feathered nursery curtains.

Because they are so broody, Banty hens reproduce like rabbits. This would be fine if they cloned themselves, added only egg layers, but roosters abound, and what to do with surplus roosters? Keep them together and they fight. Only one rooster rules the roost. The others become bedraggled, decline into depression, die. A Banty rooster in the pot is a meagre offering: no romance, little meat. All that strutting and crowing makes sinew. Tough guys to the end.

Banties are organic gardeners, voraciously eating flocks of earwigs. They decorate the lawn with plumes and pomposity. But before long, one disappears under the rhubarb with a clutch, and another struts out from the drive shed with a brood, and soon you are plagued with cockfights, and have very few fresh eggs.

Leghorns are popular with the serious egg producer. Small, white birds, they eat little and produce endless supplies of large white eggs. Doesn't matter what you feed them, their eggs are always white. Egg colour depends on the breed of the chicken. Nothing else.

Even though I know the colour of the shell makes no difference, that the inner chemistry is the same, I truly believe in brown eggs. They just look healthy, not only because they have colour, but also because it varies. Brown eggs have shades of brownness—sometimes spots, freckles even. They have character. They sit up in egg cups with authority, style.

I have experimented with different brown-egg breeds. Barred Plymouth Rocks are large black and white striped birds, plump as piebald pigeons. They're beautiful to look at, but they put food into their feathers, not their eggs. I've tried Rhode Island Reds, fair conkers of birds the colour of freshly hatched chestnuts, but again they feed their feathers, not their eggs. So now I stick with a hybrid chicken, an Isa or a Comet, small efficient feeders, who lay often and well.

Chickens are photoperiodic. They come to life in the light. It's best to buy pullets in the spring, when the days are getting long, to extend their season. It takes twenty weeks for the chick, from the time she first peeks through her broken shell, to create eggs. I've hatched my own chicks and have bought day-old chicks, but pullets are the least trouble. By the time the hatchery has them to size, they are beautiful, healthy and ready to lay. Once, a pullet I had just picked up delivered an egg on the way home. She couldn't wait, just popped it out in the cardboard carrying box.

But baby chicks are hard to resist. Every few years, around Easter, I break down and get a few day-olds. I set up a box in the kitchen and glory in their demanding peeps, their brilliant down, which looks as if it was coloured by the yolk they thrived on. They beg to be handled, fondled, petted, before they go through the metamorphosis of feathering. The children squeal and fuss, pet the silky fuzz with one finger, hold the chicks in their laps on the kitchen floor, a paper towel strategically placed.

Downy chicks are dazzling; full-feathered pullets

glossy and nubile, but the stage between the two makes the ugly duckling look like a peacock. Nothing is so bedraggled as a partly feathered chick. The yellow fades, white plumes emerge on the wing tips, and red feathers, which will become as rich as Irish tresses in the sun, grow in spotted and patchy, brown as old dried blood sprinkled anyhow. The neck grows bare, like that of a plucked turkey, and the head feathers sprout randomly, exacerbating a compromised intellectual reputation.

No sight (or smell) for the kitchen now, these unloved creatures are banished to the barn where the cats watch them frenziedly, following their moves like tennis fans. The chicks eat and grow, sip water in a crouch then stretch full up to swallow, their prickly necks inviting feline attack from behind the safety of chicken wire.

Then one day they blossom, unfurl from cocoons of mismatched skin and quill-shafts as full-fledged hens, smooth, shiny, svelte. Their heads are sleek, their necks bob with confidence, their wings flex and show perfect symmetry, unfolding like delicate Japanese fans. They strut like soon-to-be debutantes, waiting to come out, eager for the season and the marriage market. And like those courtly characters of Jane Austen and Fanny Burney, their time of adolescent grace is sweet but short. Soon they turn into Eliot's Sophy Pullet. By twenty weeks the urge to lay is upon them, and they settle into the domesticity of the daily deliverance of an egg. A chore repeated like laundry, never over, never done.

They take to the nesting box by instinct and culture. Dark and spacious, made of smooth pine and lined with straw, the box is about three feet off the ground with a small platform at the diminutive centre doorway. I cover the entrance with a piece of cloth, chintz, canvas or burlap, to give the birds the dark and privacy they desire. Their instinct draws them, but I'm sure they imitate each other, the pullets following the older hens into the box, taking on the culture of the laying hen. The top of the box is angled and hinged, and an old drawer handle is strategically placed to shed, rather than collect, the droppings of those who like to lounge on the upper edges.

After feeding laying mash, a combination of grit, corn, other grains and nutrients, as well some oyster shells if their eggs are getting thin, I take my wicker basket and open the nesting box to gather the eggs. Always it is a thrill. Some mornings I find a clutch in a pile— five or six eggs from my half-dozen hens. I find fewer eggs in the winter and in the early mornings of dark days. Occasionally there are two piles, or even more, for the box is large. Frequently I find a hen strutting about in the doorway, or just getting off the nest, her job done for the day. But sometimes I have a hen who hangs around for a while—maybe my timing is such that I coincidentally catch her waiting to lay each day. Just as

I am about to reach in and gather the eggs beneath her she raises up her body, ever so slightly, and assumes a crouch. I stand to watch as she extends her neck, raises her tail and ever so gently bears down. If a chicken had teeth, she would clench them at this moment.

A slight dip of the lower body and the egg emerges, glistening, shimmering, wet with chicken dew, pointing down into the straw. The egg tumbles and lands, graciously and safely, on its side. I pick it up while it's still wet and watch the moisture evaporate gradually but with purpose, from one end to the other. Hot in my hand, the egg is primeval, live, comforting to the body and nurturing to the soul.

First there had to be a chicken to create such a hot egg. It couldn't possibly have started without a hen.

⤙ *SWIMMING BUS* ⤚

🐦 THE SUMMER MY DAUGHTER was four, she took her first swimming lessons in town. The Alderney recreation committee provided a bus. Each morning for a couple of weeks I made her a snack, packed it in a lunch box, walked her down to the end of the lane, heaved her up to the first step of the big bright school bus and waved her off.

What I never realized at the time was that there was no particular supervision once she was out of sight. She swam only part of the mornings she was away and spent the rest of the time in the playground with the other kids, a few mothers, and other citizens of a village prepared to watch out for its children, care for its young, protect whoever was in their sight. The bus driver kept her eye out. Everyone did. And I am forever grateful.

⤛ *TURTLE* ⤜

THE RIVER IN MURPHY'S MILL is muddy, a brown body gently undulating with current, rocky riverbed and crosswinds. It cuts through the landscape languidly, like an old woman rewalking a worn path. Stony outcroppings in one bend disappear past another in a steady flat stream. It is not a river for boaters or swimmers or children to paddle and plash in. Dogs nose the water with their doggy maws, river rats ride the runlets.

I approached the bank just to park myself. To put in time, spend a calm few moments between pressures. Golden moments, valuable for their scarcity, when my children were occupied, were elsewhere, under another's watch. Stolen moments, rare as winter butterflies, and guilty moments, blissful to be alone, anonymous, childless. We seldom disclose to other mothers our powerful need to separate from our beloved babies; we seldom even realize anyone else feels the same way. I asked nothing more of the water than to share its enduring momentum, its sameness, despite Heraclitus and his dictum that one cannot step twice into the same river. I wanted only the soothing qualities of its metronome movement, its ancient heartbeat pace.

Lost in my thoughts, I looked through a reflecting lens, focusing back on myself, not inviting the water-scape in. But the creature must have moved and caught my attention, twigged my peripheral vision.

There it was midstream, sunning itself on a lone rock, a beacon, a talisman. A turtle. Most ancient rep-tile with its prehistoric green skin, its rigid carapace. It capped the rock like a mushroom. Its feet draped down, head stretched out, tail . . . well . . . its tail was short and pointed like a puppy's, but it flicked rather than wagged.

Why was it there, this buoy, this sentinel in the middle of the river? It lay still, then suddenly lurched forward, its clawed toes spread, and I thought it would disappear into the murk. But it only seemed to be set-tling into a more comfortable position, adjusting a soft underbelly to the contours of the stone. For this was a snapping turtle, whose ferocious jaws compensate for its vulnerable middle. By choosing a rock for a rest camp, the creature was protecting its belly from prey, sandwiching itself with artificial mail.

I remembered back to my first snapper. It was in the

barnyard at dusk, when the farm was young and the spring was fresh. There were no sheep then to graze and keep the yard weeds down, no children yet to bathe or rock or read to in that time before dark. The grass was long, lush and pure camouflage. I sensed the movement, the swish or the rustle. It was a warm evening, carefree; I wore sandals.

The snapper was only a hand-span away and was picking up a foot, higher than seemed necessary, deliberately, progressing forward and planting it with conviction. Startled and amazed, I jumped back before the next footfall, intrigued by the spread toes, the wrinkled skin, the steel-drum back. Until then I had seen only tiny turtles, named creatures that lived in glass houses, hid under plastic palms, fed on dried pellets. Sad creatures, who walked around their patios in circular boredom.

Here was a wild reptile. A master of the terrain. A force. A monster on a mission. I had no idea that it might be dangerous; I worried rather about its safety. Why was it up from the swamp? Would the dogs do it harm? What could I do to help?

Should I divert it? Perhaps lure it towards a water-ward track. Large stick in hand, I directed an end at the beast: no no, not this way, consider an about-face.

SNAP!

The turtle tore at the stick with one vicious lunge of extended neck and jaws. A neck on a pole, telescoping to its mark, severing the wood in a bite. Right. This is not my farm, but yours. My European ancestors go back only 250 years on this continent whereas yours predate the dinosaurs. I shall show respect. I acknowledge your right of way. Pick your trail; just let me be your guest.

It made its point, that snapping turtle, that evening in the barnyard. I am cautious now in long grass; I continue to respect its right over the land, and I have taught my children to beware. But our paths have not crossed since.

I SEE TURTLES on the road occasionally; sometimes I see them too late, after someone has senselessly mowed them down. They're not so hard to avoid, these dinner-plate Methuselahs, and it's not as if they race out on the gravel. Not like hares that zig and zag and choose the rubber rather than the ditch, or foxes or coons, which come out of nowhere at speed into the lights. Turtles plod. Their feet are not in tune with their jaws. They have the wisdom of age to ponder life; they feel no need to rush. They do not climb trees, but I have seen them dead and mysteriously placed on fence posts, legs lax with unopposed gravity.

Once, in the northland, I watched a snapping turtle lay her eggs. She dug in the sandy hollow of a huge granite boulder (a boulder as big as a bus) with her great paddles of feet shaped like serrated table-tennis bats. She worked furiously, scooping the grains with fervour, sending sand showers into the water, making her nest.

When finally she pulled in her pinking-shear paws, the hole was deep, untidy, exposed. She turned, stretched out her ovipositor and started to lay. Masses of round eggs—ping pong balls from antiquity. It took her the entire morning to spawn, after which she paused, inanimate, before sliding back into the water and disappearing, leaving her issue to its hatch or hazard.

I thought of turtles and culture. The importance of the Turtle Clan to the Mohawks. The Chinese bronzes I once saw in a Sherbrooke Street gallery: two small rigid beasts, one in the process of climbing onto the back of the other. To breed? To ride? To be carried like a new loon? They struck me as illicit lovers, heavy as clandestine hotel rooms, plodding slowly, getting nowhere, like the progress of a love that stalls on restrictions. Or perhaps they were crafted on a whim to confront star-crossed thinkers, looking for answers to unformed questions. Certainly they spoke of time and endlessness and the unknown.

Lillian Hellman writes of a turtle caught for soup, decapitated and left for the next day's chores. The trail of turtle gore in the morning led out of the kitchen, down the steps, back to the wild, sans teeth, sans head, sans life, but moving.

THE RIVER TURTLE, the snapper, was intact. Quietly enjoying the sun. It slowly moved its neck, extended to the warmth, exposed Triassic flesh draped

loosely over cold blood to the heating rays. I waited for
something more. For it to detain me in my reverie, keep
me from my role as adult, as mother. For it to turn,
expose derrière, slide, swim away. Nothing happened.
The turtle had its own time, its own agenda. It did not
hurry, had no children to collect, no animals to feed. It
may be there still, sunning in the summer sun.
Oblivious to the snuffling dogs, the bank combers, the
odd aircraft overhead. The turtle's movements are considered, pondered, careful, conserved. But don't test
them. Snappers have jaws of steel, and if you believe
Lillian Hellman, they can walk without heads.

⤛ *SCHOOL BUS* ⤜

⤜ THE FIRST DAY OF SCHOOL. Kindergarten. *Maternelle.* All day, every other day. Twenty minutes to eight in the morning until after four o'clock. A long day for a five-year-old. But she was ready. Eager and willing to clamber up the steps of the school bus, sit at the front, ride for over an hour until the school came into sight, then ride the bus again until she arrived back home, clutching paper creations and her lunch box, running up the lane, the dog wagging alongside.

We'd made no preparation for the school bus. Neither Thomas nor I had ridden one. We had always walked to school—in the days when the snowdrifts were half the size they are now and the schools were close by and the school boards were local. We'd gone to schools that had names like Fairbanks and Culloden, Brantwood and Central.

On the first few chilly mornings of September, I

walked down the lane hand in hand with my five-year-old and we waited for the bus together. If her brother was still sleeping, I let him lie; if not, he came along, held tight in my arms, as soon as I heard the bus coming up the road over the hill from the east. The red lights would flash, the stop sign swing out by the driver's window, and the wheels spit to a stop in the gravel, throwing pebbles at the dog if she got too close.

As the weeks went on, my small scholar became more confident, and I let her travel the lane by herself, waving goodbye from the open door at first, and then from the window, and finally from the kitchen table, over my tea, watching her leave for the day from a distance. Zoë kept her company, desperate to join in the journey, and more than once had to be booted off the bus, her tail between her legs, her hanging head full of dejection and woe.

It seemed an inordinately large bus with a ridiculously high first step. My daughter scrambled on all fours to get in.

⤙ *HAY CUTTER* ⤚

🖋 MUCKING TO THE BARN, the late autumn wet squishing under our rubber boots, dripping off our work clothes, my small son and I head back from his big sister's bus to feed the animals. He's rarely clean for long, and farms *are* dirt: a rich mix for growing, nitrogen for greening. He scurries around teasing the cats or playing with his toy tractors, Lego, or trucks, while I chore.

Spring's growth of hay is packed tightly in the barn. Nestled shoulder to shoulder, each hay bale lies stacked in the barn, filling the mow with the scent of sweet-grass and dried clover, wildflowers and weeds. Country perfume. We make hay while the sun shines, then feed it in the dark.

It's always tricky deciding exactly which fall day to supplement the waning pasture with a little hay, and when to bring the sheep right off the fields and start feeding out exclusively. Once I start, the ewes become demanding, forgetting how keen they were to get out of the barn in spring and onto fresh grass, how they begged and baaed as they eyed the green sprigs beyond their courtyard, refusing my argument that the pasture must reach a height of six to eight inches before they could get their first taste. By now they've chewed it all down in rotation: the Meadow, the Pie-shaped Field, the Swamp, the regrowth in the Hayfield, the Meadow, and back again around the circle of pastures. The ewes have huddled under each field's sheltering trees in heat and storm. And they're bored. They want to give their bottom teeth a rest and use their back molars. Spend their days chewing and ruminating and gestating. Let *me* be the one to forage for them.

It is routine, perhaps: the need for adventure in the spring and for coddling and a warm stable in the fall when the light grows dim. They cocoon in their thickening fleeces, grow lambs under their skin, eat for two. Or three. Or four. And I feed them, bracketing my family's feedings, our breakfasts and dinners, with trips to the barn where the menu is invariable: vegan's choice.

THE FIRST YEAR I wintered animals I had big cumbersome bales to deal with. Bales that were heavy-handed, human-handled from baler to wagon, wagon to elevator, elevator to mow, mow to stable floor. They were over a metre long and too wide to fit easily into the bale feeders we had built from a blueprint designed by a Ministry of Agriculture technician who never imagined the scope of the flying Dutchman's baler. The feeders have a square platform up off the ground and a hollow top column designed to enclose the hay, upended for gravity feed. The ewes can fit two to a side and munch through the stilts. The hay falls as it's eaten. But I couldn't lift the bales up to tip them in, and a square peg won't fit in a square hole if the bale is bigger than the hole. So I had to undo the strings, pack the feeders by hand.

My neighbours eschew knives for the baler cord. They upend the bale on the floor, push down on one edge, grab the nearest twine and pull it bodyward, to the corner and away. Easier watched than done. Then they snap the hay backwards toward the remaining twine and the bale breaks apart. Undone, it falls into thick sheaves, each compressed stack as big as a breadbox. Twines, now just ellipses of air, are parked on a nail in a beam to accumulate, to dream of a future as fence fastener or flower tie. But most end up in the dump eventually. They rot and return to the earth.

For a while I opened my bales the way my neighbours do, my time extending to fill the chore—there were no babies waiting in their beds or milling at my feet. I hauled the green brutes up to standing, struggled with the near twine, wrenched my shoulder pulling the cord off, got enough purchase to split it backwards, broke nails and got hay bites on my hands. The second twine would invariably get lost in the mess and end up in the feeder, posing a danger to the flock if it emerged around a neck or a hoof. Then my brother-in-law gave me a Swiss Army knife and I started cutting.

Over the years the bales have changed. Smaller, less intense, lighter to accommodate the mechanical bale-thrower, they slide easily into the feeders, slip down like a centreboard in a sailboat, like coal in a chute. I can pick these bales up whole, plop them in, cut the strings with my knife and I'm away. It sounds easy, but hefting and carrying even lightweight bales of hay through a hungry flock is not quite so simple. The sheep become a mob. They have no fear. They crowd and stomp on my toes and bunt each other to be first. My children are at risk from the clamber of hoofs, the forest of legs moving at speed. Sheep have no table manners. No table.

Ultimately I had to devise another method. Inside feeders helped. Long sturdy wooden racks hold a bale spread out and offer it through slats on the pen side. An eight-foot-long cribbed manger serves eight shorn sheep, or seven fleecies, or maybe six in both lamb and wool. These feeders are perfect on inclement days, blizzard days when outside hay blows into the next township, joining the odd bit of laundry that flies off the line during a summer gale. The feeders work well before and after lambing, when the sheep are divided and fed according to their fecundity (whether they are pregnant or not), and then their productivity (whether they have twins or singles) when the lambs are too small to go out. And the feeders protect my son as he runs up and down the gangway between them, or sits on a pile of straw playing with the cats who mill about his snow-suited body and bat his mittens, which hang from their strings, while he ignores the cold.

But these rack feeders are wasteful. The sheep pick out their favourite flowers and strew the stems at their feet. The stable floor gets that high-chair look—a circle of debris within dropping range—once perfected by my kids in the house. The beasts get picky in ways the bale feeders don't allow. And perhaps the sheep get lazy too when they're fed inside. They avoid having to walk.

Gravity was the answer. An old door set into the side of the mow over the stone courtyard became the perfect spot from which to pitch hay down into the bale feeders. Standing so high above the ground is treacherous, but a few boards nailed across the bottom of the opening make me feel secure each morning and keep the children from falling as I open the door to the world below and beyond. Sometimes the view is breathtaking. Framed in pine barnboard, weathered grey inside and out, the dark mow opens to a blast of natural light. The winter sun rises more to the south than the east, so is off-centre in the doorway, but the light surges over snow in an explosion of white. Sleet storms coat the trees and stone walls in fairy ice, and rain pours straight down past the opening, as there's no gutter or sill to stop its fall.

From our perch in the mow I throw cut wedges of hay, and my chubby-mittened boy launches his handfuls. We vary our pitch with the wind, and each time I score a perfect placement in the feeder I award myself two points and we cheer. A perfect score will mean a perfect day. So the bales are cut from above, not lifted, not carried. The force of gravity helps me feed, and the sheep, waiting below, look up to me on high, bestower of manna. The evening feed still takes place inside, away from night noises and dark terrors, but it is a mere snack. A bedtime soother, green tea.

My Swiss Army knife lives in the bottom of my barncoat pocket—the right-hand one—buried in chaff and bent fence staples, marbles, needle caps and sheep-marking crayon stubs. The knife has a screwdriver and a corkscrew, a bottle opener and three knives: a stiletto, and blades small and large. The smaller is my weapon of choice; string-sized, it plunges into the bale, parting stems, attacking the sisal sideways, severing ply after ply until the twine gives, snap-releasing the leaves like a spring.

For years I used this knife. I lost it once in the haystack and was lost without it. Back to woman-handling the bales, wrenching off their ropes until one day it reappeared. My knife: a blood-red spot in a sea of green, steel edge catching the sun like a diamond in a snowbank.

And for years my winter hands blanched white when I removed my mitts to pull out the blade, to snap it back. My thumbnail had a permanent break from prying the knife open. I shivered, I cut, I cursed. My children's vocabularies grew. And then I complained to a neighbour along the concession. "What you need," she said, "is a hay cutter."

Not long after, she presented me with the instrument. A hay cutter, fashioned like a miniature triangular hatchet. Her husband, McKenzie Murray, had made it for me. The handle is flat metal with a rounded end, a hanging hole, and smaller, spaced perforations along its hand-span length. The three-sided blade, as big as an elm leaf, is attached by two metal rivets, their headless ends bashed flat against the cutter, rough-edged like hand-heeled pastry. The point is nebulous, innocuous, dull. But the sides of the blade are scalpel sharp.

The cutter is heavy, and its weight draws to the bale like a magnet. My mitted hand, fat with sueded sheepskin, claws the cold steel in the way a welding glove grips hot iron. Down, like a cleaver, the string-severing blade sinks deep in green grasses, releasing them from the bale. Like breasts unleashed from binders, the bound riches relax, sag, sway and splay freely.

Twine is what wants cutting, not hay. But my cutter

is not misnamed. Once, it served to cut a swath in the field. It was a soldier in the army of blades that made up the mower. Two rows of steel triangles, set one above the other, operating at cross purposes, formed formidable teeth on the mower. The cutters rode at right angles to the tractor, ran from the power take-off and felled the standing hay in the field a row at a time. The blades were open to the sun, to small animals and snakes, to unguarded dogs' legs and fat fingers foolish enough to get too close. Vicious incisors, most of these mowers have been replaced by haybines and implements with covered blades, which are safer for dogs and children, though small rodents must still be at risk, hiding as they do in the standing sections of fields, which get smaller and smaller as the stalks fall.

Most old mowers now rust in back pastures, their sickle-sharp blades flaking and falling off in their decline. So my cutter is all that more valuable. Salvaged by my neighbour McKenzie Murray, cut by his hand from the metal cloth of a larger cloak, it feels hay in its single jaw once again. I hang it on the main barn beam, on a special nail hammered in to hold it high above curious young hands. It rests there all summer, itching, no doubt, to be out in the field mowing at the strong stalks, which are full of the juice of a sunny season. Now the hay cutter opens up bales cut by younger, gayer blades.

⤚ *BUS BOX* ⤙

⇗ OUR LANE IS NOT LONG, as country lanes go,
and affords a clear view of the road. A low cedar hedge
runs along the bottom of the garden, and a huge old
maple punctuates the gravel. The fence bottom,
though rusty and decrepit, is at least transparent, so I
could always watch my daughter get on the school bus.

Then one day it poured. Teemed down with rain too
vicious for her yellow slicker and sou'wester hat, which
was angled like a funnel towards the gaps at the tops of
her rubber boots. We got in the car, drove to the bottom
of the lane and waited there. Then all in a rush she
ran up into the bus, which had arrived just a few feet of
mud away. I realized I had not worked this through. We
needed a shelter.

The school bus wasn't always on time. A five- or
ten-minute wait is an age for a small child in the rain.
And this is the snowbelt, where the promise of blizzards

is carried on the wind or found in the rings around the moon. How would we keep her warm and dry through the wait?

Visions returned of mystery gatehouses gracing country lanes. Sentry boxes, telephone booths, octagonal playhouses, shingled shacks and horse stalls. Small constructions created, it seemed, by conscientious parents to keep their children dry and safe.

Friends who had moved to Murphy's Mill from abroad had brought their possessions across the sea in thin wooden crates. Oversized orange boxes really, but big enough for a child to play in. Big enough for a rainy-day shelter. We popped the packing crate into the back of the pickup and unloaded it at the end of the lane. It was big enough. Tall enough. Adequate. It saw her through that first winter, when most days we all trotted down the lane together in the morning. Her brother, her dog and I waited beside it in the afternoons to hear her stories of the day as we all walked back to the house together for the cookies and milk that mothers feed their young after school if they can.

But she spent little time in the shelter. It opened to the west, to the prevailing wind, which hurled sleet in the door. The crate filled with snow in a storm, leaving no room to stand.

It was a sad excuse for a bus shelter. Plywood, untreated, unstained, a rude structure, tilted and buckling from March wind and April rain, then aban-

doned in May as another piece of winter detritus,
dragged off and burned in the annual spring pyre. My
daughter was happy to sit on the rock that June, or
shelter under the maple in late spring showers. During
the summer, however, we had to come up with a solution for the following year, when she would wait for the
school bus every day of the week, and for the years to
come, when her brother would be waiting with her.

⤙ *BLUEBIRD* ⤚

⟿ THERE ARE BLUEBIRDS OUTSIDE my window.
A moving swatch of blue-violet, not quite so purple as
the Crayola crayon, but bluer than water, than indigo,
than delphiniums. Thoreau wrote that they carry the sky
on their backs, but my bluebirds are brighter than even
a Kodak sky. Flying sapphires with marmalade breasts,
precious and comforting.

Before this land was settled in the nineteenth century, my window, had it been here, would have over-
looked wood. Acres and acres (now hectares) of elms
and maples, cedars and white pines. With an abundance of trees framing patches of meadow, bluebirds
must have dotted the wilderness like wild lupines. The
fields were cleared, the cedars formed into posts and
rails, the pines into log houses and window frames, the
maples into floors and tables, the elms into skeletons.
With their nesting sites slaughtered, the bluebirds left.

Perhaps the dying elms, rotting from inside out,
first brought them back. The woodpeckers made the
holes; the bluebirds moved in. They increased,
migrated and returned. So now they are here, right out
my window, in a nesting box planted just for them in
the middle of the small side field. I can look up from
my desk, replace my reading glasses with binoculars and
frame them through the layers of glass. Take comfort in
their presence, perhaps because it is so tenuous.

The first year, they nested in an old bird box on the
fence along the sheep track. I'll never forget the afternoon I spotted the male swooping for an insect, the
sun bouncing off feathers alive with colour. I remember, because my father-in-law was here lazing with us
under the maple, grandfathering the kids. He did not
share my excitement. Not everyone is willing to give up
time to watch, discuss and worry about bluebirds.

That year was filled with bluebird elations and dis-
appointments. The first nestlings were eaten by a barn
cat. I was told (by a cat person) that the cat had mis-
taken the birdhouse for its lunch box. I mourned.
Undeterred, the birds rebuilt in a rotting branch of the
maple and I spent hours at the window watching food
go in, fecal sacs come out. Finally the fledglings
popped their heads up and down like Bert and Ernie,
more like fuzzy puppets than potential flyers.

The first cerulean male appears in April, looking
for a family home. He must arrive before the aggressive

tree swallows, who will swoop and strike. He needs
weather warm enough for bugs, yet free from marauding predators and noisy Rototillers. And then, when
finally he's hooked on the spot, he has to attract a
female. If he does, my window frames all the metaphors
of love. I watch, a voyeur of the most intimate relationship, and hope, against all my human convictions, for
traditional family values in birdland.

My children, nestlings themselves, were jealous of
my interest in these birds. There were days when they
would block my view, uncertain of their prime place in
my affections. They'd tire of my endless descriptions of
daily bluebird events. They didn't want the tally of
pieces of grass delivered or the saga of the elusive
female and her mood. Her coyness. Whether she
seemed prepared to give the male the time of day, the
treasure of her eggs. "Me, me," my children would say.

New tenants set up housekeeping, enticed me each
morning to check through the glass. I watched the flurry,
gasped when sun hit azure feathers and wondered if
Cézanne would have spent so much time with fruit if he'd
known the bluebird's complementary cobalt and rust.

One morning the female went missing. She did
not return. The next day, straw protruded from the
entrance, and I knew she was gone forever. The raccoon left clues of his crime: feathers scattered on the
ground, claw marks gouged in the post, a solitary egg in
the nest. I retrieved a feather for my desk and the egg.

Just memento mori, paradoxical blues of living sky and sea to chill me.

If only I hadn't been so smug on this side of the window. If only I'd put a collar around the post. My window framed a grave; I could have draped it in black. The male stayed for a while, looking confused and flustered and flummoxed. Where was his mate? What was he to do? How to raise a family without a mother? He left, and I saw a coffin, not a birdhouse, straw crepe around its door.

I bought a length of metal T-post, five feet of sewer pipe, stove bolts, lock washers and an angle bracket. My daughter helped me clean out the nest and my son beheaded the post it crowned with his ever-present stick. The birdhouse needed a new site, which would be framed by the mullions of my window and tilted slightly sideways to allow my binoculars to view within when the sun lined up. An old stump mound grew a new and incongruous tree of metal, plastic and finished wood. Where the cedar fence post had offered purchase to predators, the sewer pipe would repel. It was impossible to scale.

For weeks I stole surreptitious glances, moved my binoculars nonchalantly from the passing cardinals or goldfinches to the bluebird box. Finally, when I forgot to look, that lapis flash gleamed in my eye. He was back. The pall lifted and hope returned. My bluebird started to sing, to preen again. He was alone with his aria, broadcasting his availability. He was beautiful, and he had real estate.

Now even I wanted to curtain the window. After the devastation of the past it was painful to be tempted by the tenuous hope of a successful brood. I often glimpsed what I thought was a female through the glass only to discover that it was the bachelor fading steadily as the season progressed to more of an androgynous bluish-brown. The window encased a drama of soap opera proportions where nothing really happened and nothing ever changed. And my escape from the house and homework, the chatter of children and drudge of dailiness was just as compelling as daytime television is for other mothers.

When she did arrive I kept silent to avoid my family's derision. And for luck. She might not stay. Other years I had watched courting gestures become more and more anthropomorphic. He'd bring bugs rather than flowers. She'd look away and then accept. They'd rub necks, necking, and flirt and bill. Not these two. He'd fly closer; she'd move away. He'd sing on the box; she'd rummage for bugs. This was new territory. The reluctant mother, the hard-to-get feminist bluebird.

The drama continued. Act three began when she laid her eggs, after she'd acquiesced and moved in. She emerged at intervals for short sprints through damp air, or poked her head out to look for danger. Or excitement. Act four was the hatch, spread over a few days, evident by egg casings flown out and dropped at a distance by parents keen on housekeeping. This was a five-act play with a frantic conclusion of constant feeding and cleaning until the babies took the plunge and their chances with cats and coons and crows.

The avian performance provides all the romance of *Romeo and Juliet*, the adventure of *Antony and Cleopatra* and the pathos of *King Lear*. My birds do summer stock in a recurring festival, and I hold a perpetual season's ticket. Front row, centre balcony.

⤙ *FEASTS* ⤚

⟿ FEAST AND FAMINE. Livestock and deadstock. Drought and flood and everything between the two. It is all about growing: in the ground, in the barn, in the house. Venture and gain. Or loss. There are snow years and rain years and years so dry the grass scrapes the earth as it tries to grow. Blossom end rot, Colorado beetles, white muscle, pulpy kidney, cutworms, nose bots, corn borers, blue bag, thrips, scours, cockfights and orf. Pestilence, parasites and predators have all invaded the farm, but never has there been a year without feasts. Something always survives to be harvested at Lambsquarters.

The old farms weren't money-makers, but a mixed farmer didn't starve. A few cows for cream, milk to the sows, bull calves for beef, sheep to the rough pasture and chickens scratching the yard, hatching cockerels for the pot and pullets for eggs. When the price of one dropped, another sustained. And all the manure went back to the land, nourishing hay crops and grain crops and cornucopias of vegetables.

Farming goes in years. There are prosperous years and poor years. But there are also pumpkin years and aubergine years, basil years and potato years. Hot and dry makes the lettuce bolt early, but the Mediterranean foods prosper.

Long languid days, with alfresco lunches on the lawn, surrounded by delphiniums nodding in blue breezes, and hollyhocks watching with Argus eyes, half open, half nodding shut. On the pine table, covered with its Indian cotton cloth, pinks and greens meld into the garden itself: tomatoes and basil drenched in oil mixed with cheese melted by hot pasta. And the clipped grass, weeded gardens, bucolic sheep look natural and calm. As if they grew just so, with no heartache or pain. But the drudgery and downfalls of dark November days and March nights are worth every minute's anguish in these moments of bounty, when the wool money buys Chianti for the table and I sink, with my family and friends, into soporific stillness, with only the honeybees and cicadas working away around us.

Those are my favourite times, on the lawn in the sun. From the first moment of spring, when the scilla bloom in a blue lake under the lilacs, to the ancient apples making cumulus clouds on the trees, to the late lilies and phloxes standing tall, demanding sun. Even in fall, with only hardy and serviceable mums still blooming in mounds, and asters and Michaelmas daisies angling from the borders, there will be tea on the lawn. Bundled in sweaters, we still sit at the table, bare wood now, for a last time, keeping the cozy on the pot, our hands wrapped around steaming mugs with a grip usually reserved for small children's hands in crowds, drinking down the last suns of summer, before all feasts turn indoors, near fires and stewpots.

IN SUMMERS PAST we have partied up a fat lamb, sacrificed it to our friends on a spit over an open fire. It cooked all day, was brushed with a clump of thyme dipped in butter and spice, bronzed over the firepit, while the rest of the flock got sent off to the Pie-shaped Field, upwind and out of sight. It seems tactless now, with so many vegetarians about, but the taste, with cumin and coriander, lemons and nutmeg, is the essence of feasts from antiquity. The table as platter, the beast carved on oilcloth, delivered on high-piled plates with bread and wine and greens from the garden—arugula and beet leaves, mâche and romaine, buttercrunch and leafy lettuce.

But we are not the only ones to feast from our crops. One year, our best lamb was harvested from the remotest section of the farthest field by a hungry brush wolf. Coyotes are seldom seen, but often heard on August nights, howling and yelping, teaching their

pups to bay at moons shared with domestic dogs who
bay back, yearning for that wild time in their past.

Canis latrans is a medium-sized yellowish grey dogs-
body with a white belly and black-tipped coat. Looking
more like a wild dog than a wolf, it roams the semi-open
country like a sleuth rarely seen. Even by sheep. When
mice are scarce in the fall fields, having packed up and
followed the grain to the granaries and the cluster flies to
the farmhouses, the coyotes get hungry. And if the sheep
are left to roam before dawn, a coyote might strike. Low
to the ground, it edges up from the brush to steal a single lamb grazing on the periphery of the flock. The lamb,
brought down by the neck in a swift kill, lies senseless
while the flock grazes unaware.

On the morning of the wolf-kill, the sheep
count wouldn't balance. Sheep are not easy to tally.
They mill and cluster and blend and rarely jump over
fences in insomniac single file. I tried to sort them by
threes as they milled around me, but the numbers
wouldn't figure. I set off with the dog and found
the carcass over the hill, headless, disembowelled,
de-livered, unrecognizable. No ears were left, so no
tattoo could be read. I could identify her only by
checking who remained.

The coyote's feast is methodical. Acting more like a
wolf than a dog, it butchers a carcass as if from a chart
and eats the cuts in order. At second light the coyote is
off, leaving the cache until twilight or dawn.

Marauding domestic dogs do more damage. They worry a flock, chase and torment it, bite a neck, a leg at random. They kill for blood sport, not from need. A pack of dogs will leave a pasture spread like a Trojan battlefield, littered with dead and wounded, blood and gore, and the fear in the eyes of survivors lasts forever.

The township sent the livestock evaluator to determine the nature of the kill, the source of compensation. The word got out. Coyote on the north line. Willis Harris's son asked to hunt at dawn.

He arrived in darkness, positioned himself where the coyote neither sees nor smells, and waited. At first light the animal slunk back to the feast, continued his careful dissection until a shot rang out, missed, and he was gone, a blur, his prey abandoned. And while I hated losing that prize ewe lamb, the fattest and prettiest of the season, I was secretly glad the brush wolf got away. I can corral my animals, remove them from temptation. But days later another hunter drove in with his truck, the noble beast laid out in the back, his fur silver and gold and thick as winter honey, dead for his deeds. And I was meant to be pleased and to praise.

ONE YEAR, some cattle grazing the long acre (that stretch of roadside owned by the township) found their way up my lane to devour my corn crop. Beautiful heads of golden bantam, peaches and cream, sunny vee, just reaching maturity, silk forming but not bronzed, outer leaves stretching with the fecundity of their growth. Only days away from the table, from salt and butter and that melting burst of golden sugar in the mouth, sinful vegetable—an oxymoron, for how could a vegetable be evil?—and eaten in the hands, with blessings. Always I set the water to boil first, then harvest the husk straight into the ram's mouth, skein the silk from the cob and steam it. Right from the garden to the plate.

But not that year. What the cattle didn't eat before I tore out after them screaming and waving my hands like an ancient harridan, they trampled, mauled and manured. The whole crop was in ruin. Sixty days of growing for naught. Worse than naught, for my neighbour (whose fence had given, whose pasture had not) arrived with a lumpy bag of tough wooden cobs the colour of rancid butter, the taste of Jerusalem artichokes. Sinless vegetables, to be overcooked and eaten after a dour grace.

WINTER FEASTS begin at Thanksgiving when our board groans with the weight of the season's growth. Roast lamb with mint sauce, garden potatoes, carrots, squash, beans. Pumpkin pies, and apple pies made with our Spies or York Imperials. Cream from the neighbour (his cows now under control), so thick it needs a spoon to coax it from the jar. Almost everything grown at home. Nothing from farther than down the line, where some years I buy a free-range hen.

As a child I cut turkeys out of brown construction paper, added feathers of purple and red and blue, drew orange crayon legs and smiles with lips. I'd never actually seen a live turkey. We made paper cornucopias with exotic fruit—bananas, lemons, pomegranates, things we could not possibly have grown, as far as we were from the earth in that city school. Thanksgiving was a time of harvest hymns and white damask, bitter turnips and giblet gravy swimming in silver boats, grandparents sitting under engravings of their ancestors hanging on dining-room walls papered in silver and gold medallions.

My corpulent grandfather, in a three-piece brown suit, sweated with angina after too many Crown Royals; my grandmother, thin and stooped in her green dress which zipped up the back, her jewellery glittering, would be a little tipsy from her old-fashioned (after slipping me the cherry) and would laugh just a little too late at jokes she never got. We would sit decorously around the table, which I still use, and give thanks for food someone else grew elsewhere. In the worst years the gravy was made not only with giblets but with the water from the bitter turnips, which ruined, for me, the taste of everything on the plate.

I've scraped off the table's thick varnish and mahogany stain to reveal the oak—it's a table gone back to its roots. What stories it could tell of my family's feasts over the last century and a half. Now undamasked and laden with bounty grown within its view. No paper cornucopias but real vegetables nestled on real straw from the field, placed with care by my children, who share in the harvest. Potatoes: Yukon golds, Kennebecs and Red Chieftains. Gourds from the compost pile, sprigs of grain, baby corn cobs and small squash.

Each year a different harvest is celebrated. One season it was pumpkins. Seventy-two pumpkins filled the garden in a fertility blitz, and we made pies with their frozen flesh for years. One summer we had an abundance of potatoes, nine bushels. We stored mounds and mounds of the earth apples in the root cellar, with many left over for the next spring's planting. This year we have plums as thick on the branches as pearls on a string. Damsons burnished purple, tightly formed, ovular, luscious, a meretricious display gathered for conserves and jams. Fortune-telling from stewed pits rimming winter plates: tinker, tailor, soldier, sailor . . .

Lonely days of dark skies and damp air in November bring steaming pots of minestrone. Tomatoes, potatoes, carrots, zucchini, beans (green and dried), celery, parsley and my own pesto, made with summer basil, all simmer in the stock from a tough old hen. Our bones are made even warmer by our close connection with this food, food planted and weeded and tended. Food shaped by my own hands and the smaller hands of my daughter and the smaller ones still of my son. Soup sopped with fresh bread, which was punched and pulled as dough, flavoured with local honey or berries, and risen in the warmth of burning deadfall in the stove. Then formed into loaves, braids or crowns, or even animal shapes like turtles with raisin eyes and salamanders, by the kids.

THERE ARE FEASTS of pleasure and of strife. One Easter there were fireworks between courses: one guest ran to the barn in tears, too much wine, too many harsh words, and when I returned from comforting her I saw the cloud of dust raised by another couple, departing in a hurry, in a flurry, in a flight that dissolved their marriage. At the table sat my beloved, calmly serving dessert to all the children; hers, theirs, ours. Lives inextricably changed from that moment. Cousins pulled apart, parents splitting, sisters separating. Families reconfiguring as quickly as table settings, with different placemats or sets of china, or silverware. Bits of cracked crockery replaced by patterns not quite the same. Tarnished platters, the silver worn off in places, the copper showing through. Chipped crystal and mismatched glasses.

The table, which had been pulled out to a great length, became small for a time. With the leaves parked in the closet, the table ends were tightly joined into a circle. We had tiny feasts with worried guests on divorce diets. Intimate darkened discussions over modest fare: eggs, scrambled and souffléd, shirred and poached, frittataed and baked. On the saddest days, soft-boiled, with toast fingers for comfort. Farm food laid in a warm barn to nourish unhappy souls attracted here by the land itself, drawn away from the city lights and cafés by some force.

SPRING BRINGS the beginnings of hope. The first sprinkle of chives on an omelette. Asparagus. Rhubarb. Food becomes more tantalizing as it grows up around us until the summer bursts with produce, and we move back outside for cookouts, and ice cream frozen with berries from the hedgerows, there for the picking. Fresh corn dripping butter, and dogs parked at a safe distance, dripping desire. Fireflies and stars appearing late in the evening are worth braving the feasting mosquitoes. The mosquitoes' life cycle: from swamp to us to swamp. The farm's life cycle: from spring through winter to spring. Our life cycle: from child-free to parents—of newborns through youth—from peace through trauma to planting to harvest. And all over again. And again.

⤙ *FOX* ⤚

⤚ SUMMER ON THE FARM makes us lazy and it makes us diligent. The humid heat forces a slow pace yet urges wild growth and lush gardens, pastures and crops. The days are long and light. They begin early with the hoe and end late with the hose, which fills troughs for grazing animals, and baths for parched birds. And in between lie all the tasks of putting up and putting down, from planting in spring to constant harvest in summer as radishes sprout and lettuce ripens, as the first potatoes form on stringy subterranean stems, and early basil starts to shine.

Repairs seem to top the list for every facet of the farm, from machinery to windows, paint to putty, gates to rooftops. Fences bulge and bind, or give way to the constant worry of the flock and beg for wire, plier and twist.

It can be difficult to work in summer—too hot, or wet and storming, dangerous with lightning or sodden in mud. Steamy days when everything ripens and I can't budge myself from the shade or the shelter of the house, its thick walls keeping cool around me.

Children's tempers flare. They forget to share. They badger or beg to be taken to the lake, and my work must wait as we pack up and go. I watch with one eye and read with the other as they splash and swim, wear themselves out and abuse me for staying ashore, out of the marl and muck they roll in like puppies.

The summer of 1990 began with a tense sticky heat. It agitated the sheep; the ewes bleated continuously for different pasture, and the rams turned cocky and belligerent.

Late on one of those humid nights when the only movement through the window is the springing crash of June bugs against the screen, my friend Malka called. Since the day I'd followed her home years ago we had become close friends. She handspun gifts for my babies, had drawn my portrait. We gardened together. But never before had she called in the middle of the night. Her husband, her partner, the love of her life, had been driving home from the tavern when he misjudged his distance, crashed into a tractor and died.

In the week that followed, thunderstorms alternated with surreal skies of ochre light; carmine sunsets warred with cobalt clouds, and the air crackled with static. All the clocks in Malka's house flashed 12:00, 12:00, 12:00 in a neon vermilion glare as the power bounced in and out with the lightning.

Days passed with baskets of fruit and bouquets of

roses and squares and muffins and cakes and casseroles that arrived in armies, like ants on the move. A widow now, Malka ate none of it. She was quiet and alone. A space that everyone silently respected formed around her kitchen chair. People continued to arrive. They set up camp, cooler bars in the trunks of cars. Hot tempers stamped mooselike down the lane. The inevitable senseless lures of "if onlies" and "what ifs."

Everything came to a stop. The calendar in Malka's kitchen, those clocks. The harvest, the planting and thinning and weeding. The thought that we would live forever. That he would.

There was no body to view, no visitation, no funeral. Just a continuous wake moving from his home farm to the neighbour's, to the tavern in Murphy's Mill to the Alderney store. His life is immortalized by the beautiful paintings he left behind, by the memories of those who knew him well or not. My children learned about death then. Real death, of someone they knew, who was familiar and not old. How I wanted not to tell them and draw them from their innocence. The summer slipped by in a cloud.

Then the grass grew too long and had to be cut, the compost festered in the pail. Time began to move again and everyone carried on with their lives. We returned to the tasks of the season, bounty gathering like booty, needing attention. July was gone. Sand through a sieve.

FOX

IT IS DIFFICULT to harvest second-cut hay. Even without a shadow over your life. The first cut, full of thin grasses and brought in during the initial heat of summer when everything is promise and future, gets baked early in the day by a hot sun that creeps with rosy fingers over the horizon almost before night has settled in. June days shine longest and brightest; with luck they resist rain long enough for us to harvest the whole crop.

But second-cut is different. The next growth of grasses dwindles and dawdles, playing around on the ground with the worms and bugs. The legumes, however, those meaty masses of clover or alfalfa or bird's-foot trefoil, relish spreading themselves like a verdant jungle over the field, pushing their way through the cut stubs of weeds, holding each other's fronds, romancing, waving in swirling patterns with the wind. They grow luscious and thick; they hold the water and the dew. And by August the dew is substantial. It outlines intricate spiderwebs on bushes and fence wires. It lays on the ground until noon or later.

The sun in August gets tardy; she polishes her nails on the other side of the horizon, putting off her day, and ours. She is less focused on her warming task, her thoughts fixed on other hemispheres, or she mourns under the pall of late summer cloud, which gathers until the crepe sky is too dense, then falls in a shroud of rain over the fields. Drying is difficult.

The hay can be cut on a clear day, later in the afternoon. Winds are down in August and the sultry air of the hottest days is too saturated to gather much moisture from cut stems on damp ground. The longer the hay is down, the more dew it absorbs. The hay can be raked, turned over to expose its leaves to sun and wind, but there is the risk of thatching, of trapping the water under and inside until mould takes hold and the crop is lost. Rain is deadly once the hay is cut.

It used to be that hay was cut and dried, forked loose onto wagons and led to barns by heavy horses sleek with sweat. When balers came the hay was packed tightly into rectangular loaves and tied with twine. Now square bales seem to be following the haystack into extinction, for all we see are acres of huge round bales, dotted over fields like enormous cylinders of shredded wheat, bleached blond by sustained sun and thatched over to deflect weather from the precious green gold inside. These bales stay out all summer, sometimes all winter. Certain farmers build sheds for them, others cover them with tarpaulins as silver as spacesuits or sausage them in white plastic tubes. But the bulk of the bales go it alone, piled up in a field or barnyard, moved there individually impaled on an enormous poker that graces the tractor's front-end loader like an offering to Priapus.

Only an artist would envision these circular bales being carried like carrion in the mouth of a crow to feed its young. The artist, who died just as the bales were stacking in the fields, left his vision of them as part of his legacy in a mural gracing the main street of Murphy's Mill.

Because second-cut hay is so difficult to dry late in the summer, it is not usually baled in large rounds. Farmers are more likely to use second-growth to pasture their livestock or to cut it as haylage, blow it into wagons and pack it down to ferment in big bunker silos. Second-cut, scarce as it is, is the perfect delicacy for sheep after lambing. It is greener and leafier than anything they've seen since snowfall.

THE VIXEN must have been surprised at the appearance of big round bales at the edge of her wood in late summer. The night was warm, damp, but with the sun clinging languidly to fat clouds in the west. The fox was taking advantage of something unusual and had found herself a resting place on top of a bale, where she watched the sunset and pondered whatever foxes ponder.

Pointy faced, bushy tailed, the fox adapted to the field. Her ancestors were here before mine, but we have learned to live together. She stretched out on that huge round bale like Cleopatra resplendent on her burnished throne, the hay below her perfumed with the sweet smell only second-cut gives off at sunset. Herbs and berries, sweet molasses, clover honey—some combination. The few grass shards shone like silver, and the ground below, bathed in the glory of impending dusk, turned purple.

A fox prefers not to be seen. Usually it appears as a glorious brush trailing into the woods, startled from some clearing, or as a speck in the distance, gone before it can be reached. In winter snow, fox prints make a continuous, surprisingly straight track, one foot in front of another in front of another in front of another. A straight line to somewhere. But I have followed tracks until I'm tired. The foxes always outfox me. The trail goes on and on until it disappears in a windswept field, melts in a muddle in the bushes or dissolves into a thicket. Never have I found the fox. Or the fox den. Or the fox skeleton.

The vixen on the hay bale was more feline than foxy. She stretched out, inert on her high watch. I expected her pups were weaned, her responsibilities waned. Wildest of animals, she pampered and treated herself to full relaxation. I wondered how many others had spotted her there in that remote field, her legs on pause, her lashes feeling the wind, her nose still, as she soaked up the last of the summer evening sun as if the rays could pierce her heart and carry her warmly through the winter winds.

How long would she have stayed had I not stopped? Until dark? Until dawn? Foxes are chiefly nocturnal, so my vixen was just starting her day. I can't know, because she spotted me. The languor left her bones and her muscles tensed. Her ears pricked, her nose twitched. Her position was entirely the same, but her attitude was that of a mother threatened, a wren crossed, a snake cornered. We stood, eyes joined, bodies still, taut. I could win the contest by not moving first. I lost the encounter. For she fled. Into the woods and away. Another mystery in a summer full of confusion.

Dusk fell.

⊰ *BUS HOUSE* ⊱

⤙ AFTER THE FIASCO of the packing crate, split into its various veneers by the weather, caved in and warped, and looking like nothing better in life than a packing crate to begin with, we dispensed with a hut for a time. I sat in the car in inclement weather, both kids now perched on the edges of the seats, ready to hop out at the sign of the bus, their backpacks trebling the depth of their chests. There are no neighbours close by. We tried not to feel shame.

Not every farm has a bus house, and few kids seem to seek shelter in those that do exist. You see siblings milling about in the rain or sliding in snowstorms, their backpacks on the roadside, their dogs jumping about, their shelters empty. But for many rural dwellers, bus houses are overt indications of kid care. You need to let the world know you are prepared to provide some space for your children to wait, no matter what the weather.

Eventually the need to provide for his family got to Thomas. That and the need to build something—anything—so he could go and buy new wood. But like all of his projects, the shelter was not made without salvage. He found an old door (a very old door), tall and made of narrow tongue-and-groove, with a beautiful ancient glass window that distorted everything seen through it, including the school bus, which appeared to swim up the road in a wave of motion, humped like a porpoise in paint. He used old two-by-fours, still fully two by four and mined from the back of the drive shed, and cedar shingles left over from the roof. He salvaged the small mullioned window from the loft, for light from east and west.

When construction began, the children were still quite small. My daughter was taller than my son, though he was always taller than most kids his age. We'd been marking their heights on the mud-room's door frame on every birthday and half-birthday since they were steady enough to stand. Pencil lines grew up the bare pine board like the rings in the tree it came from. At first I had to crouch down to make the line.

It was one of those warm weekends in September when we pretend the days are still long and we ignore the crickets chirping the season out like a warning Greek chorus. One of those Michaelmas daisy weekends, when their magenta and mauve heads hang heavy with late dew, nodding along the fencerow. One of those *schadenfreude* weekends, which turn on you for no reason, resent your good will and suddenly blow cold and windy. The crickets retreat and the masked chorus takes centre stage, its utterances muted by Aeolus.

Up early, off to the lumberyard for boards and battens, the kids strapped into the jump seats of the truck. Home, by way of the Alderney Feed Mill, then coffee and the Saturday papers. The work began in earnest when the dew had dried and the chickens finished their egg-laying cackles. Their work done as ours began.

The kids carried nails in a box and tools. Saw and hammer, and hinges harvested with the Victorian door from some fancy dwelling. They begged to ride in the wheelbarrow, but it held the shingles and window; there was no room for them. Stones formed the foundation, laid flat at the corners, solid as rock to build on. The base was boxed with two-by-eights, and the floor was laid on top. Then the frame rose. And rose. For some reason Thomas built his shelter up into the sky until it blended into the maple tree. No one could say he was negligent now.

The weather grew cold and the children lagged and whined, bored with the chore of finding and handing, the game of hammering their own nails into useless board bits. They dallied and dithered, moved ever farther from the site until they found themselves in the house, begging for hot drinks and food. But their father soldiered on, framing and siding, battening down the battens, boarding the shed roof. By the end of the day the structure was solid and steady, ready for finish and trim.

Next day the shingles went on, layer over cedar layer. The door was hung, the window set, and it all smelled wondrous and fine. Sap from the pine, musk from the cedar, must from the Victorian door. Oil in the hinges and the fresh reeking earth dug round the base. Two chairs, pressed back and bent, their seats dubiously split, their paint thickening out their patterns, fit side by side in the house. Marshalled up in neat rows, like the desks in old-fashioned schoolrooms, so the kids could wait in eclectic style, sheltered, dry and safe.

⤙ *BEECH* ⤚

⤜ NATURE HIDES DEATH, conceals its horror
under blankets of flaming leaves, thatched grass or
feathered snow. Nature lofts ashes skyward or floats
them away on liquid currents to dissipate, dissolve,
transform. Nature offers refuge too, places that draw
us at times of stress, soothe us in any weather, absorb
the evil humours and give us back our selves. My solace
is the magic beech tree.

Architects call what can be seen beyond our own
borders "borrowed landscape"—that expanse of view
over the fence or across the street or beyond the back
lane. In the country these boundaries are already
blurred. Line fences have no signposts, and we are usually welcome to stray across them.

Realtors indicate farm boundaries from the road
and point to fencelines. A sweep of the arm encom-
passes forest or field. But no agent walked us over the

farm. We owned it before we saw it all. Perhaps we haven't really seen it all yet. Certainly not learned it all. The Pie-shaped Field, the Hayfield, the Meadow. The Swamp and Bush. The Sidefield.

The cedar fences that bound the farm are snaked old and tight, their rails weft for geriatric trees that first poked through as sapling warp. They herringbone the underbrush, the elms and maples and chokecherries, the apples and mountain ash and lilac. And the wild grape entwines a triple helix around the twill.

After carefully walking within our property, we ventured across to the neighbours' for our first trip over the fence. A rock-pile corner at the high spot, back beyond the Hayfield at the northeast boundary, makes the fence accessible in the tangle. But with no trees for support, the rails slant to the north, pushed by the snowload to tilt down the hill.

Once we get over the fence and through the trees, we view a scene that resembles a Renaissance painting. Hills and trees frame the space, drawing the eye to the middle distance. Permanent pasture falls away, with no particular paths to follow, but the direction is clear. Forest and hill off and away, water in the middle of the canvas, rolling fields to the left, dipping to flat grainland, then wafting up to the coagulations of glacial moraine. To the right more valleys and hollows, where the ice lingered then charged, scraping and gauging and leaving granite calling cards. A perfect elm beckons on a height, and a sea of fall colours contrasts with the few white pines still standing. Mystery in the patches of forest beyond. We go that way. To wear a path.

Down through the field dotted with purple fall asters, thistles and teasels, we climb over a sagging fence in the far corner. Below is a spring, gushing from the bank like Niobe's tears. It pools, hesitates, narrows and falls to swamp below. Wild watercress still green amidst the dying edge grasses. Water clear and cold as ice wine.

A lane levels the rise above the stream and leads upward to the next field. The grand vistas suddenly enclose and become contained spaces bounded with hillside, wood, swampy bush and fencerow. At the gate, scrubby pasture undulates to the south and east, broken rails sharing lichen with carbuncular rock piles and dried raspberry canes. But the lane, the tractor path, the cattle walk, whatever this track is, leads through a wild orchard. Hawthorns, bare-leafed now, expose empty birdnests and vicious thorns, fruit cemented to branches. Long stiff grasses and starched Queen Anne's lace, burnished goldenrod and faded chicory, its blue flowers clouded by frost. The track leads down towards a wood, then up, to shaded space.

And without any warning it is there. Off to the side. Magnificent. Alone. Enormous. The magic beech tree.

The atmosphere instantly changes as we are drawn off the track. The crown is so dense that even leafless, it filigrees the sun. The beech owns the high point.

Refuses neighbours. Like royalty, it demands distance as if cordoned off with gold underbrush. Nothing grows under the spread of its boughs. Clad in the palest grey leather, bark without nap, it is elephant, sleek seal. Its knots are elbows, heels and the puckered orifices of breathing things. Its limbs are animate, waving and stepping and fingering the earth.

High on a natural pedestal, the tree demands the reverence of an upturned eye. Praise almost. Druids may be charmed by oaks, but I am compelled to the beech cult. Beech. In German, *Buche*, from the word *Buch*. The tree was named for the books made with slabs of its wood. I see a lifetime's reading in its leaves, gathered at my feet now, but the beech is poised to bud again with endless new chapters as the seasons turn like pages, faster and faster with time.

The tree should not seem so remarkable. Virgil gave the beech homage in his *Georgics*, so I've been warned. But the massive trunk, short but thick, gnarled but smooth, sends branches that dance from its body like arms from a Hindu deity. The curve of its bark makes muscle of wood and sinew of twig, and fecund bellies erupt on all sides. The tree demands to be circled, checked for *trompe l'oeil*. Exotic already, it soon reveals an anomaly.

One of the largest branches has grown off to the west and then somehow formed an umbilical line back to the trunk. It is a living, growing, connecting thing. Or has the trunk reached out to the branch? It is impossible to tell. The trunk seemed all of a piece until we found this flying buttress of bark stretching like a strut. Or a guy wire. Or a lifeline.

From that first day to this, the beech remains an enigma. Slate blue, it swims in a sea of its own. Far from a line fence, park, village, or mooncalf with a penknife to enclose initials in a heart, the tree stands alone. Looking out over some private demesne. And I am a supplicant.

If sometimes, as Frost claimed, life is too much like a pathless wood, where an eye weeps when hit by a twig, there are also rewards for struggles through the bush. There are those who do not care to forge new paths. The magic beech is not for them.

But this tree is both ore and lore for me. I've climbed its branches, stretched on its boughs. I carried my children to see it when their eyes were just newly cracked, then later helped them climb it themselves, small booted feet sure on its silver limbs. Countless picnics, successive dogs, triumphs and sorrows were all marked by the ceremony of this tree. Special friends taken to it alone and severally. In through the wardrobe. Part of the secret. Hidden knowledge, like that of the leaves themselves, which were valued by early settlers for mattress stuffing, prized for their springy comfort so superior to flattened straw.

Were leaves gathered from this magic tree? And

drawn by horse and wagon in burlap bags back to the farm? Did women rake and stuff them into waiting ticking covers, striped blue and white, shyly stained and noticeably bleached? Pack mattresses full to coddle backs stiff with winter milking, sore from recent harvest, flexed with cold? Use them as soft shelter to conceive magic children or sweetly scent a sick bed?

Each season the path changes, and with it the magic beech. In winter, I glide over the Hayfield, manoeuvre the fence with my skis in the air, or trickily sidle up to the rails, straddle them with one ski over and to the east, one still to the west, make a quick turn of my body with the second ski aloft and I'm across. I telemark down the hill and, in a good snow year, sail over buried barbed wire to the spring, carry on up the rise, pause at the top and search for that snowshoe hare, so well blended and difficult to spot. I ski downhill through the orchard and herringbone up the hill at the end, or skirt around the knoll and along the ridge. The latter gives me a longer view, but the former gives the sudden shock of the tree, white capped, iced, like a Florentine figure released from marble.

The beech holds my attention each time I visit, but I get chilled and must keep moving. I make a snowplough turn down the hill to the pond, check on the open water, then set off through meadow lanes two farms over, passing field after field to the forest where I'm under cover of sleeping maples. I get to the road and then home for hot wine or cider or buttered rum. When I'm on skis the magic beech is too close to be the end of the path. The beech is the beginning. It draws. It beckons.

In February, the first thaw. Rain making mud. Dogs sniff sleepy coons, brown and rank, from their lairs. Crows gather: black on a grey sky. From the slick stride of the ski to the slog of the boot. Black on brown. Field stubble dead and buried. The magic tree looms outwards, its branches fanged. A cartoon tree, haunted, sinister, sleek and black in the wet. Inhospitable tree, too slippery for muddy children to climb, but not to be ignored. Magnetic still.

Finally spring. The wild leeks take their chances under the beech's branches. The air is pungent and fresh, warm hints on the wind. Buds furled and bulging are coloured like anachronistic businessmen in polished brown brogues with light grey suits. There's time to linger. The children hang like lemurs from the branches, each trying to outdare the other. The path's end. We spread an anorak as ground sheet, unfold a mouse-eaten table cloth, and open the hamper of food. The first picnic of the season, to be followed by feasts among the trilliums, the wild violets, the marsh marigolds and the harvests of hay, then grain.

Late summer, after the barley is off but before the corn is ready, when the cicadas sing and the jays gather and the geese begin to *ka-ronk* and fly east and west,

west and east, thinking of the trip south (picking their marshals and testing their feathers) we set out again, knowing that the neighbour's bull is safely in the barn and the grain is in the granary. Our last beech lunch of the year. Sultry day of September, grasses dry and scratchy, crickets looking for scraps. The children, bigger now than I am, still climb to their favourite spots while Thomas and I lie back with our hats on our faces. The old dog sleeps, the puppy waits at the base of the tree. All of us are refreshed by its strength and are drunk on its magic.

⊷ *PLOUGH AND HARVEST* ⊷

🖎 FIELD WALKS COME TO A HALT until after harvest, which drones on well into the autumn. We must keep to the edges of the fields and with summer's full growth on fencerows there can be little space for travel. Then, before the last cornfields are combined, deer season begins. The hunters herded up from the south don't know our migrations and peregrinations. I stay inside and watch from a safe distance.

I was once told by a classmate about a poem by Keats on ploughing, though I can't find it in any concordance. It could be a rural myth, but rural myths don't tend to run to Keats. I first heard of the poem in my student days, when I wrote about pigs in James Joyce. "The Boarding House," a story in *Dubliners*, is full of swine imagery, and I called on my farming lore to note it. Gilt just means gold-plated to most readers. But every farmer knows that a gilt is a young female pig.

A gilt to a sow is what a heifer is to a cow, that saucy teenage stage before the first lying in. So I realized the metaphor of the golden clock on the mantel, the nubile daughter suddenly pregnant, the boar hiding in the ding house. And my rural colleague recalled the Keats poem.

It hinges, he claimed, on the trajectory of the plough, round and round the field to the centre. But that's not how the plough—or the harrow or the double disc or the haybine or the corn planter or even the combine—travels. It's never that simple. Perhaps Keats, if he wrote such a poem at all, dreamed his ploughing picture, watching the nightingale rather than the lark.

The method of striking into a field, whether to open it up or clear it off, has always been a mystery to me. Fields are ploughed and planted in rows. You can see the furrows between the crowns, thick gullies between clods of rich earth, almost black in November greys. The furrows glisten in frost, are snow-rowed in winter, hard-packed and regular with the turn of the plough. Each share on the plough cuts into the earth and angles down. The mouldboard lifts and turns, flicks over soil the way a spatula folds cake batter, tunnels ahead leaving earthen gullies, running crowns. Still, fully formed, the field is armed from the ground for wintertime, when nothing new grows or feeds. The grasses, stover, weeds or stubble are sent to the underground. They descend into darkness and wither, deracinated, disjointed and dead.

There is pleasure in making the furrows—practised far from the road by the novice, in fields landlocked and safe from neighbours' eyes. The patterns are visible only from above, where hawks search the fencerows for mice, or seagulls focus behind the plough, diving for unearthed and bisected worms. Only when the skill is perfected will the plougher move to the roadside field, daring to put the results on display. There is pride in a straight furrow. Pride in all the work of farming. And every fall there are contests. Not just big ones, where implements are drummed and business is done and the whole of agriculture seems to turn into a marqueed mall with muddy floors, but also small matches on individual farms. Heavy horses and single-furrow ploughs. Reins and harness and rubber boots. Rain and toques and jostled arms as the shares dig and slide, the mouldboards turn the terrain, and the jolts of the horses, the stones, the inclines and declines move up through the hands to the tendons and muscles of well-veined arms, still tanned from summer chores and roughly calloused from constant use. And almost every roadside field is a contest. Every furrow is on view to every pickup truck driving by. For farmers notice, they observe, and they take note.

I DETERMINED to learn the pattern of fields. The flying Dutchman duly arrived while I was at my desk at the window, overlooking the field so close to my own. The leaves gone, the sky bleak, my work innocuous, I took up my pen and paper and plotted a graph of his route. I took up two pens, a blue and a red, and began to draw the pattern of the field on the page with arrows for direction.

A pitchfork in hand, he paced an eighth of the way into the field at the top end, stopped, and dug in the fork. Back to the tractor, he paced again from the lower edge of the field with a stake (a broken hockey stick, its telltale tape intact) marking a straight line from start to finish, from stake to fork, fork to stake. Between the road and the first cut into the land he left a space of grassy stubble, wide enough for turning the full length of tractor and plough. "Headlands," they are called, and they are two-headed beasts, guarding the field at both ends. The plough does not travel round and round to the centre, but manoeuvres the headlands to return to parallel lines, up one side and down the other of the field.

The first cut appears where the ploughman decides to strike out. Discs ahead of the plough, or iron blades in times past, cut into the earth for the share to enter and the mouldboard to turn. They are called coulters, and they precede every blade of the plough, act as gate-keepers to the earth, keys to its locked thatch of summer vegetation.

My grandfather's name was Coulter. Coulter McLean. He was born two generations away from the plough: two after, for his grandfather was a farmer, and two before, as I came back to the land only a county away from the homesteading MᶜLeans. And I wonder if he knew that his name meant more than the relative he was called after.

My neighbour's is a five-furrow plough. Five coulters, five mouldboards with five ploughshares: one a piece. The mouldboard is not a board at all anymore, though once it would have been made of oak or elm, the iron share bolted on. The Egyptians developed the plough from a crude hand-held stick into an implement pulled by animals, and the Greeks added wheels. In times of war Hellenic ploughshares were co-opted, their iron shaped into weapons. Ares led the fight while Demeter mourned for her lost daughter. The land was idle, the grain neither sewn nor reaped. The plough just a distant constellation in the peaceful night sky.

With his Dutch heritage, my neighbour can take pride in his shiny plough; its prototype was conceived in Holland in the Renaissance. With a slimmer shape and lighter coulters and mouldboard plates, the plough was easy to use and inexpensive, making it popular and available. My neighbour, when he came to Canada, brought his history with him, having ploughed with his horse as a boy, the reins tucked under his arm or over his shoulder, the shares skimming through the low nether land devoid of rocks.

When he arrived in the township he was told the

field beside my farm could not be ploughed. Impossible. That first year he marked every rock, every boulder that broke a shear pin on his plough, and the field was dotted with stakes like an apple orchard newly planted with saplings. It took a backhoe to dig the rocks out, one at a time, and they filled a swale in the pond-field beyond. One by one he dug them out and dropped them into the bog, where they sank down through vegetation to disappear forever. Or until the next glacier.

He pulled the rocks and he ploughed the field. And he's ploughed it every year since; after seasons of grain, then corn, now grain again, oats and barley mixed, budded or bearded and swaying in June winds, feed for his cattle, bedding for his sheep, golden sheen for my eye on summer mornings when dawn's rosy fingers reach it first on my eastern horizon.

HE EXPLAINS it all to me now, how the plough works, where shares meet mouldboards, how the coulters cut through the tangle of twitch and milkweed and stubble of the field floor, and guide the share through the newly sprouted grain, turning it in the furrow. He tells me about the dead furrow, that double gully where divergent directions of the plough meet. One side of the field moulds the furrows to the right, the other side to the left. When they finally meet, the furrow deepens, widens, forms a split in the field with no crown. Crownless, the furrow is dead.

His plough leaves a sixteen-inch track, more than twice the width horses could manage, their strength limited, finite. Their feet an average seven inches wide, they pulled ploughs with furrow widths of six to nine inches, and when the seed was scattered it fell to the notch and sprouted in rows just far apart enough for the horse to walk through. When the cultivator weeded or the binder harvested, the horse could lead without stepping on the crop.

Horses are now packed by the hundreds into powerful diesels, their four-foot walk turned into four-wheel drive. Twenty inch rows, on twenty-furrowed ploughs— wider than equine imagination. Monsters you can't buy new for twenty thousand dollars, and can't sell used for ten thousand. With new innovations the plough might go the way of the horse, only brought out a few times a year, testament to a past when the land was new, unbroken, resistant, but made to yield to that cutting edge.

While my Dutch-born neighbour takes pride in the cut of the share, the turn of the mouldboard, the straight furrow laid even from south to north, in easing his plough over the *geeren*, that triangular section inherent in an uneven field that no English word names, the sixth generation Harris boy wants only to make the earth black. There are no prizes given for fancy ploughmanship in the daily chore, and he is disdainful of what he calls "recreational ploughing." Like his grandfather before him (an excellent farmer, an infelicitous ploughman), he takes off the coulters, drags cornstalks in a braided rope of bedraggled dross, their gold spent and gone, paid to the combine in dues. The way of the future is to conserve the earth with no-till planting and save fuel with fewer passes of machinery. Yields increase as the years pass. The plough sits rusting in the yard, its shares ironically craving dirt to make them shine.

A third neighbour, whose ancestors first opened crown land, who farms still on the fields claimed from the forest by his grandfathers, prefers to plough in a tractor with an open cab, needing to hear the sound of the plough, its music. He uses a three-furrow plough, and drops the *d* in the mould of his boards, visualizing them as moles running through his fields. And he bemoans the destruction of earthworms, regrets their dissection by the shares as he cuts through the field, and indicates his intense connection with the land. Involved. Implicated.

HARVESTS STRETCH through the season. Winter wheat is planted to root before the dark days underground, spurt in spring and be reaped just after hay, the very first crop to come off the fields. Spring seeding happens early in well-drained land. Tractors ply the furrows or drill the stubble; the weeds are turned under or chemically euthanized, their enzymes inhibited, photosynthesis blocked. The browning of Canada. Haying starts with the first growth spurt, when the grass jumps overnight, the legumes unfold their fronds and the earth allows the forage harvesters to traverse its surface, which is still unstable from deep frosts and spring runoffs, sports stone patterns where none lay in fall. The haylage flies from the spout, augured from below, and sails into covered wagons, small boxcars that trundle up and down the roads, now empty, now full, back to the home farms to bunkers or silos. The herbal tea ferments and condenses, fodder for livestock who lick their chops and salivate at the scent.

When the fields are dryer, hay is baled, either square or round, thrown or stuck, tossed or piled, tied or sheathed. The sound of the baler each sunny afternoon, *chunk-a-chunk-a-clunk-thwap*, sings late into light-filled evenings.

But the grain harvest is somehow best when you can watch the old ways as we did when we first arrived in the area. The binder and stooker across the road, the sheaves tied and plied, small idols to Demeter, fair bouquets pointing skyward. The grain in a spray on strong straw stalks, waiting to be threshed on the barn floor and winnowed in a wondrous display of grain from chaff.

LAMBSQUARTERS ISN'T big enough to grow grain. The sheep need our fields for pasture and hay. We can improve our pasture by fertilizing with manure and by rotating the animals from field to field to keep the weeds down and the grasses healthy, but our hay periodically needs to be replenished. Legumes don't live forever.

When we first had the Hayfield ploughed, we seeded it down with alfalfa and timothy, but underseeded with oats and barley, a thin mixture, which would jump ahead of the hay, shelter it from hot sun, nurture it along and crowd out the weeds. It is called a nurse crop. Before the legumes had time to blossom, the grain was grown, tall golden strands, their heads swaying in a progressing wave with each heavy gust of summer wind.

One of the Harrises came in a combine to harvest our crop. The header cut into the swath, winnowed out the grain, augured it up into the bin and left the straw behind in windrows to be gathered later and baled. And when the gold was gone from the field, the green began. Small plants unfolded, the grass grew straight, and before long the mix of clover and alfalfa blossoms purpled the green like crown jewels. It lay in the field, finding its feet, not to be harvested until the following year.

The grain filled one side of our granary. But the storehouse's tin lining was thin and worn, and the rats found their way in, brought their friends, their relatives, and moved beyond the barn and into the house that autumn. I was shocked by the sight of a large brown rodent on the basement wall, and Thomas was horrified at the thought that his home was invaded. He felt lax in his duties. The exterminators were sent for, the rats done in.

CORN, THE NAME for all cereal grains elsewhere, is native in Ontario, distinctive. Here the maize gets tall enough for mazes to be cut through it. The academic agriculturalists once said it wouldn't grow in our area because of the elevation, and the heat units it needs. But it just grew taller and closer to the sun in the township fields, defying the experts and delighting the raccoons who raid the fields for cobs. A late crop, corn takes longer to get past the green stage than wheat or mixed grains. We watch it grow in our neighbours' acres after their other fields have been harvested, ploughed, put to bed for winter. And it has various uses in the vicinity—cob corn stored in cribs, or silage hunkering down in a bank bunker—but much of it is grown for its kernels, pure gold nuggets of cash crop.

I had never been in a combine. I had driven the old Ford 8N, ridden the wooden seed drill, spent more time than I'd have liked on the hay wagon. I wanted to experience the harvest for myself, so I arranged to ride as a passenger in the Harrises' huge John Deere, which was as green and gold as the crop itself and a couple of storeys high. Just around the corner from home I found the young farmer harvesting the perimeter of his great-grandad's field, for the combine starts on the edge. He's a tame titan of a man, who loves his work but is always ready to chat. A sixth-generation Harris, whose two baby sons make the seventh. His aunt, whose corn it was, climbed down from the rig, grinning. "I always like to ride that first round," she said. "It's the only one I get all day, what with bringing the wagons back and forth." And the combine drove up to her tractor, poured out its first silken crop, ribbons of peach melba as the corn flew unfocused from the bin and out the chute of the monster machine into the grain wagon. She hauled the wagon away when it was full, to unload at her home place.

I climbed up the combine's ladder, into the cab and gazed around and down. So high up, the hills rising and falling in the distance, the autumn leaves brash in the woods, the crop crisp and dun ahead in the field. And inside? Shocking state of the art. A glass bubble, quiet but for the cell phone, the CB, the radio and the computer, the bells and whistles of measurements being taken, yields being assessed. The GPS gave our coordinates, the elevation, the size of the field, the amount of corn coming in, its density and dryness—it was all there on the tiny screen in the corner. Each field is named, its details held on disk, and the information is fed into the machine on top while the corn slakes the combine's thirst below.

For harvesting wheat, the header (the part of the combine that first connects with the crop) winds round like a Ferris wheel, rolling the grain and straw in together with each turn. But the corn header is coni-cal, with seven huge pointed cylinders that look like barrels that have been turned into dunce caps; their green metal points aim between the rows, guiding the cornstalks into the machine like flies into the web.

Unlike the plough, the combine starts with the perimeter and does rounds at first. But then it strikes out into a section of the field. How does the farmer know where to enter? Which row does he aim for to separate the stalks into the six spaces between the points of the mechanical header? After leading me to believe he had some extra sense, some innate knowledge of corn growth and field division, young Harris confided that it was there for the seeing. There is a slightly different width between the end of one edge made by the six-row corn planter and the beginning of the next. So the crop is hex-sectioned in the planting and subtly marked for harvesting.

There were no horses needing solid ground and turn-around space, just this huge machine doing elephant ballet in the field, four wheels driving together up the hills and power-steering effortlessly through three-point turns. An edge of the field slinks into a gully, which might have trapped a horse, stuck a plough, but the combine drove its seven metal snouts downwards, sniffed up the corn and sneezed it out as chaff on the field, crop in the hopper. Backing up, we saw the area was clean and stovered, uniform with the rest. And if there were stalks missed? Well, we went back to them, for even flattening them out makes them look right from the road.

My farmer can't leave a field partly done, so he worked until it was finished. Took his breaks when the last wagon was filled. I climbed down, and off he went to another farm, another ten or twenty acres to clear, to open for the deer. They would enter his sights in the following week between harvest and plough, when the farmers, always rising early, would expose themselves to the elements all day long and call it a holiday.

⤙ *WINTER PARADE* ⤚

🪶 ALDERNEY IS A VILLAGE lined in maples. In fall they burnish a brilliant red arcade over Main Street, contrasting the yellow brick of the buildings. A river runs through the village, is dammed upstream to form a small lake, bounded by a wooded and grassed park with a ball diamond and a pavilion. When we first arrived in the area Alderney had two gas stations with mechanics, which dwindled and were rekindled over the years with various managements and incarnations. A blacksmith, now gone. Two churches, which survive and thrive. The General Store. The Feed Mill. The new school. The old school.

The General Store is facetiously called the Alderney mall. Farmers meet in the back there each morning over coffee, not that there is a back really, just an area between the aisles near the freezers. It serves as a kind of morning tavern. Ladies (with escorts or not) stay near the front of the store. Hellos can be volleyed, but I wouldn't walk back there unless I needed something specific.

Successive owners of the store have had their own characteristics. The first owner we encountered, John Feather, never took pennies in change, but rounded down to the nickel. "I thank you," he always said, and from the first we felt welcomed. His leaving was a sad day as his successors were a grumpy couple from away. They didn't last long. Then Ron and Fiona jumped in headfirst, took the place on and made it their own, revived the sense of spirit it had almost lost. But Ron died and Fiona couldn't manage very long by herself. So now we have new owners and everyone is breathing a sigh of relief because they haven't changed anything much. A few racks are on new angles, there are condoms near the cash, but the atmosphere is the same, the contents continue to amaze and the hours of business are constant.

Weather is always the opening subject. Particularly in the winter when we rush in for supplies if a storm is threatened, or when we finally return after a storm-stayed week. Weather is central to farming, though, so it is crucial in all seasons.

Late fall is stable. The harvest is complete. The local kids are well set in school. Hunters gather at the store for coffee and chocolate, cigarettes, extra gloves and maybe a lottery ticket, hoping to bag at least something on their quest.

Once the hunt is over, preparations begin for the last hurrah on the calendar. Alderney's parade is not your usual commercial Santa Claus parade, which starts earlier and earlier each year to persuade people to shop and spend; it's a festivity harking back to times before the advent of tractor-trailers and multinationals. You can see the parade revving up by the number of horses out on the roads, drawing carts and wagons up and down the hills and through the village. Practising.

The Alderney area has a Mennonite community, so horses are always evident. In Murphy's Mill there are hitching posts at the grocery store, the medical centre, the bank. We see horse-drawn buggies every day, open and exposed to torturous winds, their occupants riding beneath sideways umbrellas, their faces red with weather. The children who cannot fit on their parents' laps in the front, ride in the storage area behind the seat, facing out and wedged in tight. The girls' blue bonnets frame their fair faces, their braids pulling taut. The boys are ruddy, capped and shy. Older members drive in the covered *Dachwaggeli*, a square one-seated box of a buggy, which gives them a little more protection.

On Sundays they form black queues on the roads, dark horses pulling darker buggies filled with families in mournful clothing. They form a sedate procession and recession to and from their Old Order church. But later in the day, when visiting is the custom, you can see young men cantering their horses, flicking the

reins in play, or catch a glimpse of adornment in the
green pinstriping on certain polished carriages during
courting. Risqué, this display is tolerated to keep the
young men in the fold, to maintain the community for
the future.

Other horses roam the township roads in summer,
their riders capped in English or western gear, or
muster herds of cattle from their summer pastures
down the Sixteenth Concession back to their home
farm on the Second. Good-looking cowboys, their
oiled coats splitting over their mares' or geldings'
backs, hold loose reins over the pommels as they guide
the edges or get in behind the beasts, looking down on
the summer-fattened stock with pleasure. By winter
their horses are back in their stalls or running in pad-
docks newly sprinkled with snow.

But the heavy horses are what I suddenly notice as
they memorize the road in early December, preparing
for the parade. Percherons and Belgians, a Clydesdale
or two. Massive rumps rippling as they pull bright red
wagons through the village. Empty wagons going
nowhere at all. Just back and forth, stopped by the Feed
Mill or the General Store, turning at the school or the
township shed. Clipping and clopping while the cars
whiz by and the old guys gather near the bench or at the
garage, remembering.

The horses practise their strutting, anticipating the
crowds of Christmas. Everyone comes to the village

parade. There are no trucks or tractors, no motors at all in the parade, just mares and shanks' mares, mules and miniatures, donkeys and dogs, Arabians and camels clomping their shod hoofs or cloven hoofs or paws on the road, huffing steam in the air, ringing sleigh bells on their traces, clanging brass on their harnesses, sporting antlers on their canine ears, pulling carts of children and carollers, trees and presents, queens of the fair and men of the year. Outriders trot, elves give out candy and mounted police place holly in their harnesses. The churches sell baking, soup and cider, and friends will feed us cake when the procession is over, their house nestled over the ravine downstream from the dam, but just feet from the road. We'll be freezing by then with the waiting, the watching, the search for our neighbours' Percherons Bud and Duke and the glorious matched mules who come from afar. We strain to hear the pipes as they play by the store, fearing they'll march silent as they pass by our spot. And every year Thomas feels guilty when he sees how few pipers are in the band, their knees red and cheeks puffing, their fingers blue on the chanter blowing "Bonnie Dundee" or "Aiken Drum."

For there was a time when he piped with them, wearing the tartan of my paternal great-grandmother. Played her name, "Maggie Cameron." Played "Dornoch Links" and marched to "Speed the Plough," "The Road to the Isles," "The Skye Boat Song" and

"Flowers of the Forest," a lament. He was the solo piper
at the wake for our late friend, the painter. He played
"Amazing Grace" again and again into the night. When
the children were small and he had more time, he
would practise in the field, the pipes much too loud for
the house. Then we would attend weekend parades
both here and away and our blood stirred with the
tunes, which were some innate call to the heather, the
heath, the sheepfolds of generations before us, some
link to our pasts blurred by highland clearances and
lowland war brides, sad farewells and fraught crossings.
We're caught still by the music, haunted and stirred by
those nine notes, those drones, those slurs and dou-
blings: the *Leumluath*, the *Taorluath*, the *Birl*.

Now Thomas stands in the crowd with us, fingering an invisible chanter, breathing rhythmically, but
the pipes lie at home in their box, the one he built,
lined with tweed from the isles. The drones are braided
together with homespun dyed in the reds, greens and
yellows of the plaid. Every year the kids pester him to
promise to take up the pipes again and every year he
does promise. Perhaps next year he'll play.

The band marches by our family, the floats clip
along, the animals bask in the opportunity to work, to
display, to carry their keepers, pull their loads. Huge
shaggy hoofs with massive steel shoes, steaming horse
buns making small children giggle, against the back-
drop of snow and frost and toe-numbing tempera-

tures. Everyone is shivering, laughing and stamping. The sense of community is as sharp as tears stinging watery eyes, raw as noses red from exposure, warm as hearts reaching out with the sense of giving, of caring, of taking in the scent of the season right here. Close to the ground, close to home.

⤙ *STAYING* ⤚

⤞ THERE WAS NO QUESTION of not staying here, right from the start. We'd tried the city. We'd tried the country. We liked the country better. I guess I'm prepared to spend time with myself, though I do crave the community of friends. And I never quite fit the mould but am always outside. On the margins. The edges and sedges of life.

When we travelled across Canada we learned about the country's disdain for Ontario. Prairie dogs resented our privilege, West Coasters chided our weather, Maritimers couldn't help but be kind, but they branded us still. Ontario seemed the place to stay, as here we have no apologies to make. Home. Where our ancestors—from the eighteenth-century Scots surgeon to the United Empire Loyalists, the nineteenth-century English gentleman to the post-war orphaned babies, the rugged Highlanders cleared from their land to the powerful Chippewa matron at Michilimackinac—all chose to stay.

When we first came to live on the farm we maintained our city contacts. Symphony tickets and theatre, regular visits from friends from afar, and trips away to see them too. But the work got under our skin. It burrowed in and left its mark, deep lines and brown spots from too much sun. Biceps and bulged veins from too much hefting. Broken nails and dirt stains from arms in the soil, digging and planting and making things grow. Tomato plants staining hands green and walnuts making them brown. Callouses on palms and heels from the fork and the spade. Machinery branding a crescent moon on one arm, breaking bones in the other, raising constant bruises on my body. Wind blowing my hair into tangles and straightening it out, or rain curling it. Sun bleaching and drying and splitting and carving deep lines into my face. And anxiety doing that too, and illness and loss of sleep. For there is much to care for with beasts in the barn, bairns in the house, the worry of wood and of well. The crops from the garden, the hay for the flock, the manure to spread on the land. The manure smells. Reeks. Permeates the house and gets right into my hair. Even the butter picks up its taste.

The power goes out. Or it surges and breaks our equipment, our light bulbs. Lightning hits with regularity. And we wait for repairs in the dark. It's cold in the storms, when the wind heaves power lines. Woodstoves are fickle for heat. The logs must be cut, year after year and split and moved and stacked and dried. Then moved once again to the woodshed, restacked inside. Then brought in the house, a few sticks at a time, sloughing bark and chips in a trail. The wood feeds the fire, which is hungry for more, and more and more. And I get tired hauling wood and stoking coals and taking out ashes and tripping over the scuttle in the garage where the cinders cool until we can spread them somewhere safe, where their heavy metals won't harm.

But it is a real fire heating our home. The sweet smell of apple or lilac follows the cedar kindling that Thomas splits into thin faggots that crackle at the first touch of flame. Then solid maple or elm or the weed smell of ash filters out our chimneys, drifting smoke across the field and into the bush, back where it all began.

The mornings are chill until the fire is lit. My loft is like ice while the embers brew and make up their mind to heat the chimney bricks, which gradually take on the warmth and then release it to radiate and caress. This heat makes me stay.

ISOLATION IS palpable. I feel it in the great handfuls of nothing sifting through fingers trying desperately to grip. I feel it in the disjunctions between my past and my present. My silver pepper mill at odds with my shitty boots. I never quite fit in here with the families who have been in the township for centuries.

I GO TO funerals and weddings. To showers in the village. Every young woman is feted in turn and everyone comes with gifts. Wonderful gifts, sincerely given, and we sit in chairs in rows in one of the two church basements and watch the bride and her bridesmaids. Her mother and her grandmother. Each gift is passed around, row to row, and we read the card and ooh and aah at what others have brought. Afterwards there is a game to be played: we use the bride's or groom's name to give bits of advice.

> K - kiss every day
> A - always make up before bed
> R - reach out for each other in times of stress
> E - each child is a blessing
> N - never give up on each other

And I find myself unable to play, wanting instead to change these ways, give a reality check.

> K - keep your birth name
> A - always have your own bank account
> R - read about marriage contracts
> E - enter with caution
> N - never give up your rights

But I delete before I write. Except about the bank account. Just as a hint.

The funerals are usually in Murphy's Mill, because the Alderney churches aren't big enough. But we go back to the village for a lunch, which is served by the ladies. Sandwiches and squares, tea, coffee. There is no chance to mingle as we sit at tables. In rows. We talk, or not, to whoever is beside or across. About the weather. About whatever. And I see, as if through a window, the sense of community here. The layers of family—babies on the floor, toddlers at the table, parents and grand-parents—all here to bury the great-grandmother who has lived here all her life, as her mother did before her. And I feel like a stranger. An outsider. And I realize I can never fit. Not really. And still I stay.

I try to understand. To learn about the needs of farming and to accept the progressions and changes. But I abhor it when the farmers bulldoze the rail fences and mow the trees down in a trice so a bigger machine can get into a roadside field just a few times a year. And I walk through the snow to the man across the road with the saw, the fellow on the bulldozer, and I cross my arms as he says good morning. "Just how many of these trees do you need to take down?" I ask. And we com-promise on a few and I apologize, not wanting to be one of those city people who replace the For Sale sign with No Trespassing or No Hunting, or both. But I see it differently. Those hand-hewn rail fences are spilt like toothpicks with one swipe of the dozer; the borrowed landscape is ripped open and scarred for years. And still I stay.

November and February and March. Those are dark months of sleet, wind and mud. The fog. Where weeks on end are grey and greyer in Grey County. Where the ceiling is so low the sun never appears and the blue of the sky is bleached into wisps of memory. Slush on the roads and ruts in the gravel, washboard before all the stops. Nothing is clean or easy, and it seems better to stay right at home; to eat the food in the freezer, the cans in the cupboard, the roots in the cellar and the jars on the shelves. Going to the barn is the biggest trip of the day—and sometimes the most resented too. Hungry animals, baaing their needs, meowing their discontent, clucking their disdain if I'm late. I throw out the hay, fighting the wind, and miss the feeders and sprinkle those precious fleeces. I drop a bale from the mow and graze a moving kitten, who *merowzes* in pain and indignity. The water overflows and floods the stable. And the sheep need rubber boots to keep dry. And I break down before fixing it. Wondering why I'm here. And I stay.

The lives of my children, teenagers now, are complex and intricate and away. Their friends are not close by; they must drive to see them, and that adds hazards of its own. Vehicles crash into icy ditches, are write-offs, yet they walk away. Not all are so lucky and the sorrows start. Three schoolmates killed with guns. Self-inflicted. And illnesses take two more. A snowboard kills one and carbon monoxide another, and the favourite teacher drops dead of the shock. It's like war. Sorrow in battalions. The flag is at half-mast most of one year, and how do I comfort my children for that? How do I reconcile living in this place, which makes so many so desperate? And I watch my daughter and son age and mourn and learn from experience way beyond their years. And I grieve. And still I stay.

Just before shearing, as I'm preparing the barn, I fall backwards over the shearing board and bring the heavy sheep scales down on top of me, breaking my arm and trapping my legs. I'm all alone; Thomas is away. I fret I won't get free, but somehow I do and totter outside to plunge my bent arm in the snow. I pull my watch off my swelling wrist and call for help. And of course it arrives. The flying Dutchman, driving more slowly than I've ever seen, carefully delivers me to the hospital after buckling me into the truck like a child. The Harrises send help for the shearing, which goes on without me, and clean up the mess I left of the barn.

The nurses all know me, and the doctor too, who takes time after the X-ray to order me dinner before he heads down the road in an ambulance with trauma so very much worse than my own. I lie in emerg and friends arrive, and then thankfully Thomas. He holds up my arm (my March break) for his colleague to cast hours later when the ambulance returns from the city through the snow.

Finally spring comes with its thin reeds of hope. Light thickens and lengthens. Lambs arrive and fill the days and nights with work—awkward work with only one hand to help. Earth appears through the snow and finally greens. Healed. And I'm still here to start it all over again for another year. Staying.

⤙ *HELEN* ⤚

⟿ I NO LONGER SLEEP in the barn during lambing. I have extra responsibilities in the house and
away—my children and my work—and I have tried to
breed a flock that can lamb without my help. No longer
Hampshire crosses, with their bullish heads and necks,
but sleek Border Leicesters, their snow-white Roman
noses built for birth canals, their shoulders supple
enough to slip through a pelvis, their bones fine and
elegant. But still I check on them. I stay up late; I get
up early. Some nights I set my clock if a ewe looks
imminent. For still I cannot suffer losses, and if I'm
there to help, the losses rarely occur.

I never get used to the miracle of birth, though I
am so conversant with the process that little phases me.
There are variations certainly. If the cord breaks over
the lamb when it emerges, blood will spatter on the
tight new wool. Rich scarlet spurts over fresh white

hide. I've learned that the blood is just the remains from the umbilical cord, thin blood vessels stretched by the journey breaking naturally with the tension. The blood comes from the placenta, not the lamb, and not really from the ewe either, as the cotyledons begin to detach and the afterbirth sloughs away. But it can be frightening for an uninitiated observer. Blood equals danger equals fear.

The lambs themselves look different depending on the amount of amniotic sac still clinging to them, on the waxy material within, or on the presence of meconium, the first feces, which the lambs expel before birth if there is stress. The lamblings can be stark white, solid yellow or speckled brown. And occasionally they can be as black as the ace of spades.

IT WAS THE SPRING of the school exchange. We hosted an Inuit boy from the north and the trees amazed him. The forests. And though he knew every-thing about hunting and fishing, about slaughtering wild beasts for food, he knew nothing of farming or the cycle of life in sheep.

Our northern visitor arrived during lambing. He watched a pair of living twins being born in record time with little fuss or confusion. But he was disturbed by the sight. Disgusted even. Sickened. He had to leave the barn and was reluctant to return throughout his stay. Perhaps he sensed disorder. Perhaps he knew all was not as it should be. Certainly he contributed cultural assumptions different from our own.

The mother was attentive to her twin lambs, but indeed something was wrong. Where the ram was sturdy and getting sure of himself, valiantly trying to reach his feet, nosing his mother for first food, the little ewe lamb was floppy. She couldn't get herself up, despite her energy and determination. Spindly and spastic, she flopped in the birth waters like a boat-trapped trout. She contorted and twisted and tensed, all her synapses working at odds. The suck reflex was there, but she needed support to feed.

My son joined his new friend in the house. Thomas silently shook his head. My daughter rolled up her sleeves and helped me deal with the new one, dry her off, hold her up, ensure she got a bellyful of colostrum from her mother. We involved ourselves in the immediacy of the work to delay the concern and put off the solution, just focused on the problem at hand right there in front of us. Every few hours we went back to the barn to check, to assist in her feeding. She was eager, she was hungry, and her mother loved her. A survivor.

THE BOOKS call it "daft lamb syndrome," a typical veterinary descriptor like blue bag for mastitis, or black leg or pizzle rot. Unlike human medicine, which revels in obfuscating meaning between practitioner and

patient, animal disease talks plain. At first I wondered
if the lamb had a case of swayback, with her twisted neck
and permanent glance over her left shoulder. For the
first few days she could not stand at all. I had to help
every few hours, day and night, to hold her to the teat
and let her suck. Most farmers would have thrown her
on the manure pile; she had no future as a breeder.

Over the years I've lost and I've saved many critical
lambs. Cold and weak newborns, barely breathing,
have come into the house in towels under my barncoat
to be put by the wood stove, propped on a hot water
bottle, dried with the hair dryer. I've fed them brandy
to boost their energy, colostrum through a tube, or
with a syringe if they can suck at all. I've had precarious
little beasts revive, bleat, shake and stand on wobbly legs
in their box, graduate to a child's playpen when mobile
and accept the humiliation of disposable diapers with a
hole cut for the tail.

The successes are enormously gratifying. But they
are mixed with many failures. The lamb left too late.
The one too cold. The pneumonia that gallops ahead of
the antibiotics. The sorry of spirit.

When I was pregnant with my own children, we
lambed early to have the ewes' labours over before mine
began. But the cold was vicious and the losses were great.
I'd trudge with my big belly to the barn, lumber over
gates and crouch awkwardly to help. I'd question my
adequacy to mother when my ability to shepherd was

impaired. More than once, the house sheltered babies of both species—in and out of wool—all in diapers.

Finding a dead newborn is devastating. Not attempting to revive a weak one is unthinkable. It might have been easier, when my children were small, to dispose of moribund lambs than to have them die in the house, hear their death rattles and watch their muscular fasciculation after they gave up the ghost. But disposing of them is not a possibility. Sometimes they recover. I have to try.

Despite the wonky lamb's grave problems, she had the determination of a coon raiding the feed room. She would tense her muscles and will her survival, founder and fall and finally flop up onto unsteady feet. She was able only to circle to the left. But she was up.

I left her with her mother as warmth wasn't a problem and I couldn't risk her rejection. I believed she would learn to feed herself—negotiate a path to her mother's teat, latch on, stay and suck. But whenever she got close to the udder she'd continue in a circle again, away from the very thing she longed to capture.

The dam felt confined in the small pen. She stomped, wanted out. Her patience waned, as did mine; no longer would she stand while I held the squirming lamb to suck. I got out the bottle.

Helen, as my daughter named her, for Helen Keller, took to the bottle. She stiffened and shook, spilled and sputtered, left as much milk on us as inside her, but she wanted to live, she wanted to eat. With wool matted around her neck, she smelled sour. But she charmed like a heartbreaker, a beauty, a Helen of Troy.

She thrived on her feeds and tied me down to a schedule in the barn and a chore in the house. Sheep's milk has more fat than cow's, so I buy a special powder to feed a bottle lamb. The formula mixes poorly with water, making my kitchen a mess of blender, bottles and spills. A lamb needs six feedings a day for the first while and is not like an infant human, who nuzzles the breast in the warmth of the bed and is returned to the crib across the hall or stays to snuggle until morning. Artificial lamb feeding means alarm clocks in the house to heed needs in the barn. I must wake, dress in boots and heavy coat and mix the gloppy mess of coagulated milk. I warm the bottle in a beaker of water, distrusting the microwave to preserve nutrients, and carry it sloshing across the yard. The journey is dark and cold, but the silly broken lamb's delight paid dividends. The sleepy flock, too, squinting from the light, entertained me with yawns and stretches, chuckles and bleats. Ewes lying down, their lambs on their backs or tucked into their flanks or under their noses. Little family clusters arranged within the pen. Helen stiffened on my lap, her rigid muscles in constant flex. But her good eye shone with pleasure and her mouth worked away.

In spring my son visited the Arctic, set out on a snowy journey with his new friend and learned the details of the hunt. At home, dealing with the domestic, I tried putting daft Helen out with the main flock, but she couldn't cope with a six-acre field. When the others came into the barnyard she lagged behind, travelling in circles, oblivious to the rules of direction. In the tiny Sidefield, which is less than an acre and narrow, she could navigate crookedly along the fence to straighten out her circles, and find me or my daughter when we brought her bottles, which dwindled down to four a day, then three, and finally two. Her path through the pasture was patterned like a pulled-out Slinky, around and around until, after overshooting, she finally connected with the bottle and sucked it dry, snorting and huffing and making it her life's work.

Her hunger woke me every morning, and her gratitude rewarded the early rising. She was always ecstatic to see me in my ratty coveralls, pulled on over my nightshirt, bottle in hand. Helen marked the dawn and the dusk. She woke the farm and put it to bed with her baby bleats, reminding me daily of possibility and promise, of conviction and tenacity. Her head was sideways, her legs crooked, and she had about as much stability as a drunk walking a line.

I watched her all that summer. She listed wildly to the left and her front legs were misshapen and misdirected, splayed and awkward. She grazed, but on a tilt, unable to compensate for the earth's curve. A flat-earth lamb. Between steps she looked almost normal, her head askew, puzzled, working out a problem. Her belly was distended from the bottle feeds, her muscles lax, her wool lank. She couldn't see with one eye. But she ate, she grew, she felt the sun on her back and gave no sense of being censured. Her mother answered her bleats, and her brother encouraged her grotesque parody of gambolling in the evenings, when lamb devilment peaks.

Even after weaning, Helen needed the fence to guide her to water and oats. She spent the autumn with the other yearlings, avoiding the truck and the market. When the ewes were bred, I let her run with the flock, certain that the ram would avoid her, leave her alone. And he did. She spent the winter in the barn, moving back and forth with the others to the courtyard for fresh hay each morning. She found herself a spot at the manger for grain, sidled up to the water bowl, nuzzled into the straw each night and slept her crooked sleep. She never straightened out, never learned to walk without a list, never mated, lambed, nursed. But she gave us all her special favour of attention; she was tame to anyone who cared to pet her.

My shearer just glared at me that March. Then softened and lovingly removed Helen's wool, which was matted, she thought, from an inability to shake. The undersheep. Kept, not killed. Helen found her spot in the flock, as mascot, touchstone.

By spring she was still going in circles, but had mastered the art of the field. Always last to the barnyard, Helen could almost keep up. She no longer needed a small space, and the new crop of lambs played with her. She began to fit in. No longer falling over, she could jump with the others. She was a springy sideways creature, barrel-bellied and contorted, fun-loving and carefree.

But what about fall breeding? Helen couldn't foster lambs. Couldn't hold still to feed them or find them or keep up with them. That was a problem I never solved. One morning in October, just before Thanksgiving, Helen lay sleeping in the fold. But as I approached her, I recognized the ultimate sleep. Not a sign on her, not a clue. Just lying dead, muscles finally relaxed. She was so calm and unbent, I had to look over the others to be certain it was her. Helen, that daft lamb who flopped into this world and fought her way through, died in her sleep overnight amongst the flock she learned to graze with.

I clipped some fleece that day. Just enough to make something to remember her by. It lies in a basket, lofty and white, waiting for the perfect moment, the right project, the distance I need to touch her again. So she will once again touch me, as she did the moment she spilled into the world, thrashing and gasping. A wee bent animal, terrifying to behold, but full of the most remarkable frustrations and pleasures.

⊰ *RACCOON* ⊱

🐾 AFTER THE THANKSGIVING bounty, after the glorious sunsets of Indian summer, when fall merges into winter and the cold rises and the days diminish, the sheep stay close and the summer animals disappear. The groundhogs go under and the coons find their dens. Chipmunks bed down in subterranean condos. There is time to reflect on the passages of the year, on the visitors, the parasites and the thieves.

Now that my children are in their teens, I remember back to my own youthful days. I watch them interact with small children, with animals. I dread telling them of Helen's demise, then marvel at their acceptance, their energy and their patience. The summer I was fifteen, I looked after my cousin's children in Muskoka, as a mother's helper. She taught me many things: to drive, to make jam, to sail, to think very hard before having babies. There were adventures, a couple of love interests, a lot of frustrations and a baby raccoon.

Its mother had been killed—there were no details. The baby was a mere suckling. And because I was desperate about animals and deemed responsible, I was designated to care for it. I filled a baby bottle with milk and sat on a kitchen chair with the coon nestled on its back in my lap. My first soft nursling. Its four rubbery feet wrapped around the glass, its eyes closed wistfully in their black mask, its belly bulged. It sucked, grew, was weaned, became snarly, was released to the wild.

My next contact with coons was in Montreal in the form of an antique coat. It must have weighed more than the combined poundage of the poor souls who made it up in those days before boycotts and spray paint, but it braved blizzards and the deepest snows I'd ever seen. And I wore it to shreds.

Grey County is serious coon-land. Every farmer has stories of raccoons found, raccoons dispatched, raccoons trapped. On the rafters in the hay mow, my first coon here seemed harmless, beautiful, sleek and exotic with ringed tail and reverse purdah, only its eyes hidden. Days later I stumbled on the nest in the hay. Four perfect babies, identical, tiny and trusting furballs, happy to be held and coddled. I replaced the bale but returned each day to inspect, to hold, to show them to my children, defying the cautions of their teachers about animals in the wild. It wasn't long before the denlings snarled. Bared their teeth and let me know I was a stranger, as they had been instructed.

My relationship with raccoons has spanned many years. And if it's a competition we are in, the coons are winning. But I do not submit. The battle is one of wits. And of tenacity. When raccoons move into the barn, they do so not just for shelter, for birthing mangers and sweet-grass suites. They also crave food for their growing broods. And my feed room is a coon buffet. The cat food is their favourite. The small circles of dried protein, fat, flavour—cat Cheerios—tempt others besides my feral mouser and tame tabbies. If the cat food is left in a bag, the coons chew the corner. If it's put in metal cans with childproof lids, the thieves open the lids and tip the cans. Bungee cords sometimes work. Sometimes not. The coons eventually undo the cords with delicate hands and help themselves.

I find solutions though, am ever innovative. The cat food now sits in an old diaper pail with a fitted lid wedged by its own handle. But the pail can't sit on the floor. Instead, I suspend it from the ceiling, hang it on a stretched-out coat hanger from a spike in the beam. I bump into the pail and have to detach it each day to feed the pusses. I have to explain it to visitors, this white pail embossed with a golden nursery lambkin that has the nose of a dog and the eyes of a rag doll, swaying in the middle of the room.

Other feeds are more difficult to protect: the oats

in bags and bins, powdered molasses, laying mash. I feel like a locksmith some mornings breaking the bonds of the tinned and bungeed feed as the rooster crows, the hens squawk, the sheep bleat with impatience for their breakfast. And so I resort to the trap.

For years we had just the odd invader, and a borrowed neighbour's trap would do. We'd use it once, transport the offender to barren land in the next township and let it go. But we've become, I believe, the great raccoon repository for the province. The rural Rocky dump. City coons have come calling in slick summer suits in recent years, delivered in traps from the wilds of Etobicoke and Scarborough, Rosedale and Forest Hill. I've purchased a trap of my own.

But if, as I suspect, these are swaggering city slickers, plantigrade on pavement as well as turf, they are also trap-wise by now. I picture them working my barn in pairs, one holding the door of the cage while the other ventures in after the marshmallow. Sometimes perhaps one goes it alone with a ballet step, a hind foot elevating the spring-door for eventual exit while the front hand extracts the bait. It can take days to catch one. I find the barn cycloned, cans tipped, grain spread, cat bowls toppled. And the trap tripped and empty. No bait, no coon.

Squirrels are easier prey. One March I transplanted an entire colony of red squirrels in a week's trapping. Peanut butter was their bait. They walked right in—to their immediate regret and unending protest. Local folklore has it that a squirrel must be moved at least nine miles away and across a river. I sent them in all possible directions in this multi-streamed county. The great squirrel diaspora. They will be telling their grandrodents of it now and for ages to come. But they've stayed away. Made room for an infestation of chipmunks who live in the ground at the base of the squirrel-den cedar trees and pop their heads out of nowhere like periscopes, dodging dogs, tempting fate.

Chippies run along the six-lane highways of the rail fence, the dog in pursuit, changing lanes faster and with less warning than a black Trans Am. More than once, I've found one trapped in the top of a hollow log, the dog on hind legs sniffing her doggy breath into the hole, prepared to park there for as long as it takes. But rarely are chipmunks caught. In the barn their luck lessens with the feline hunters, and more than once I've found nothing but a tail lying on the feed room floor or draped over a cat bowl.

But coons outflank cats. And most dogs too. There are legends about farm dogs dispatching masked strangers, and I've seen young coons shaken by their necks to their death. But an adult coon scares most dogs. Even coon dogs stop at treeing, satisfied with their role of finding and directing, but leaving the dirty work to the guns.

I can't kill a coon myself. I see them waddle away

from their mess, amble up the stairs to the mow if I visit the barn of an evening. Easy prey if I were armed. But I can't do it. My father taught me to shoot a rifle when I was twelve. We shot targets and tin cans, and I got pretty good, shouldering the butt, setting the sights, easing the trigger. But I don't use a gun here. Wouldn't think of it. Can't do it.

Coons have anthropomorphous behaviours that make them difficult to hate. Their feet have five fancy toes, their hands five nimble fingers. Inquisitive and daring, they are thoughtful with their food, washing fish in a river, examining morsels, turning and investigating each tidbit before eating. The raccoon's English name is distilled from a Native word, derived from the Algonquian family of languages, variously recorded as *arakun*, or *arocoune*, *arathkone*, *aroughcun*, *rahaugcums*, *rarowcun* meaning "he (or she) who scratches with his (or her) hands." In French it's *raton laveur*: "young rat washer," "young rat who washes." The raccoon's walk is as delicate as its wash—hunched, like a daddy-long-legs planted high and round.

One spring evening I saw a coon sitting on an unused chimney on the house. A nest. (Confirmed later by a climb with a flashlight, which illuminated five pairs of small eyes shining up through the dark.) I looked roofward on that first spotting; she looked down. No fear. As if she knew her safety was assured by her batch of babies. Bold, she ambled over the gables, nibbled on the wooden windows, scratched at the shiplap. And when asked not to, she merely stared, considered, and crept away.

Working late in my loft, catching the last of a June day that streaked orange tongues of sunfire on my desk, I was aware of a presence. There are small Gothic windows on each side of the loft, which open on our shingled lean-to roofs. On the east side was the coon. Standing on the shakes, her hands gently pressed against the screen, she was peering in with myopic nocturnal eyes. Her belly was that of a nursing mother. Six teats, pink, erect, with matted fur around them, pressed flat by suckling babies who would be full now and sleeping in their own lofty nest. She stared hard at me. Mother to mother. She dared me to evict her.

For six weeks she tried my patience. And ate my house. I thought perhaps she chewed the wood for its savour, so I put blocks of salt on the ground at her entrance, a low point straight under the sunroom roof, which she climbed down slowly every evening, peering through skylights and windows on her way. The tenant nodding to the landlord. I yelled at her, lobbed a football in her vicinity, threatened, pleaded and cajoled. She stared with big black eyes and went on chewing. Ignored the salt. On hot evenings the babies appeared, lined up along the upmost edge of the chimney bricks, stretched languidly and slept. Caught the cool breezes from the west. Like lodgers in undershirts, swilling beer on city porches, belching, oblivious to neighbourly decorum. I don't know if they played on the skylights while they lived here. I've heard they use them for slides in the rain. A water park for the wild.

Finally they all came down for a move to larger quarters, for an introduction to barn raids and cornfield parties. Things calmed down for a time. No further gnawing of house wood, no terrorized cats, no grain upset, no early corn torn in the garden. The raccoon family must have headed off to the woods, the streams, the lush cornfields in the distance. Grass is greener.

But by midsummer they were back. With a vengeance. With a grievance. And nothing could keep them out of the garbage cans of feed, the sealed bags of grain, the leftovers of feline kibble. Every morning the barn was a mess of flung containers, spilled metal mouths spewing forth onto dirty concrete, muddied and manged by ring-tailed critters. Out came the trap. Marshmallows disappeared as fast as I could set them as bait, and almost no one was caught. Occasionally I'd get one. Hunched in the trap, looking deceptively small and sweet, but heavy as heartache to lift and smelling rank and musky and vile. I put the trap on newspapers in the back of the station wagon, opened all the windows and headed out to someplace that needed coons. Across a river. Nine miles of scent glands to freedom. Freedom from and freedom to. Each time thinking the problem was solved. Each time having a few days' grace before the next attack.

But then the raccoons crossed the line. They tore open the chicken pen. Pulled back the wire with deft hands. Woke me with the squawking screams of panicking poultry and made off with two of my buff Brahma beauties, prizewinning hens just into their lay.

Worse than wolves, the vermin took more than they needed. They were greedy, relentless, violent. And when I spied a great large male asleep in the Russet apple tree in broad daylight, I called a friend who has a gun. She came. All my pacifist ideals blanched as she shot him out of the tree, finished him off ("they don't die pretty") and left me with the carcass, already attracting flies, dead on its back, bloating.

I hauled it onto the trailer behind the tractor, drove it to the back of the farm and dumped it before the kids got home from school. Body disposal. Unworthy of the coroner who would be sure to find it and determine the cause of death as acute lead poisoning. To the head. Raccoon patriarch. Paterfamilias. Dead on his back.

There are hard choices on farms some days. If you have livestock, you will have deadstock. But that raccoon has been my only kill. My neighbours would be horrified to know that I trap coons and let them go: I contribute to the menace. But I've discovered peanuts. If they're wedged into the very inside edge of the trap, the beasts have to go right in to reach them. Peanuts will not be coaxed or rolled like marshmallows. Peanuts stand their ground. They get their man. They get my coons.

All is quiet now. Christmas coons den down, sleep in soggy skins rank with the odour of the unkempt. Matted and dozy, they appear on warm days but do little harm before burrowing back into fouled and fousty hollow trees. But like butterflies fresh from their chrysalises, raccoons will emerge when the days start to get longer. Sleek and crisp, their masks saucy come-ons, their tails like those of lemurs, they'll start the cycle again. Females will mate with handsome males, find my barn, investigate my chimneys, drop their young and feed on whatever they can steal. And we will continue our game of cat and mouse, trap and trick, and for the most part, we will co-exist.

↞ *POULTRY PODIATRY* ↠

↠ THE CHILDREN ARE ON HOLIDAY, and the chickens, like the residents of Cairo who go to Alexandria for the season, are in their summer residence. In Egypt, Cleopatra's home lies underwater, drowned in time and washed away in memories, which only surface in the odd flash of gold. Here, the chickens' Cairo is submerged, awash from a leaking water bowl, making chicken-shit soup in the barn. The coop has been reinforced since the coon capers, Fort-Knoxed to protect my hens and their gilded eggs, and the raccoons have retreated from the echoing blast of the neighbour's rifle. But a leak has formed a silent and sudden spring on the floor, and the chickens have been removed to higher ground, to a cooler place, to their Alexandria.

As they strutted around their winter residence with its flooded floor, their feet gathered balls of hardened guano, big as eggs. Clogs. The chickens could step dance. Each day they were more heavily shod, higher booted, platformed, pattened and stilettoed. Some feet looked tidy as riding boots, others messy, laces dragging, tongues hanging out. The latter being the sort of chicken who would carry its wallet on a chain from belt loop to pocket. These chickens clicked when they walked with their tap shoes and beat out a tattoo in the nesting box, an ostinato.

The clogged feet might have been a trick, like prisoners feigning disease. Or a decoy setting me up for a surprise. A Trojan horse. I tried to ignore their clunking claws. I waited for the warming window sun to bake their boots off, for the waters to part, for someone to fix the leak, for a miracle. I shamefully put off dealing with the megafeet until it approached cruelty to poultry. Finally I was compelled to take action.

My daughter, though she is not a hen lover, pitched in and helped me catch them and perfect pullet podiatry. We grimly gathered our tools: secateurs and penknives, screwdrivers and scissors. The day was warm, with the promise of summer, the threat of languor, the possibility of malaria breeding in that swampy floor. The hens needed the cooling breezes of the coast, the dry security of an outdoor run.

There is no literature on chicken pedicures. Debeaking, caponizing, sexing, inseminating, banding, plucking, roasting and fricasseeing all have their established techniques. Chicken housing and raising and butchering can be learned from books. Even chicken glasses are in the literature: putting little red-lensed spectacles over their eyeballs will stop cannibalism. You can read up on that. But not foot problems. Chickens aren't generally caught in floods (unlike turkeys, which are legendary for not coming in out of the rain). They high-step and strut. And scratch.

Chickens are usually fed from hoppers that are raised to beak level and filled from above. The feed elevated from the floor mess stays clean, dry, wholesome. But chickens love ground food. They'd rather scratch the dirt, peck a piece of cracked corn, scratch some more, uncover a bit of barley, turn around, bend from the wishbone, tail in the air, and scratch—left-right-left, peck a piece, right-left-right. Barn hens, even those running loose, get few pecking chances. Cement is adamantine. It just doesn't yield to the debeaked bill, doesn't conceal or cover grains and fibres. Outside hens pick a scratch patch and attack it the way cedar waxwings strip a currant bush. They strut and scratch, bend and turn, peck and nod until every speck of food is gone.

As a child I had a chicken toy, a pecking toy, coloured red and yellow and apple green. It was made of wood and string and had a red-handled square paddle. At each corner stood a little yellow hen and underneath were four separate strings, which met at a red ball hanging below. If I started the ball swinging, the chickens would bob and peck at the paddle, painted green as grass, and alternately connect their beaks with the yolk-coloured specks of grain. I spent hours feeding those hens, preparing for my undisclosed farming future. But they didn't have feet. They were pegged to the board, to the strings. No scratching; no chiropody.

But these birds are real. Their feet were as rock-hard as a gangster's on his last trip down the river. With our mining tools ready, we stuffed a bird headfirst into an old boot to hold her still, contain her beak and wings, so that we could gain access to her feet. The first hen was very badly off. She'd met with some string, caught it around both feet, pulled and pulled until it was noose-tight and she wound up hobbled. Two toes were so badly covered with muck they were stuck together. I cut them a little too close, adding to the confusion and mess. But my anaesthetist bravely stuck it out—two women running the farm—it had to be done.

The boot made a poor container. It held the bird, but she couldn't breathe properly, was terrified, claustrophobic perhaps, compressed. So we improvised with the chicken catcher—a piece of number nine wire, the farmer's friend, with a catching loop at one end and a hanging hook at the other. After snagging a bird around the ankle (do chickens have ankles?) we hung her from the rafters, upside down, wings awry, beak on a dangle, feet up and exposed, ready for the clippers. We could have used a jackhammer.

One by one the chickens emerged clean-toed and ready for their new pen. We worked together, my daughter and I, to convert the old outhouse by the drive-shed into a chicken hut with straw, a roost, a laying box and a fenced yard. Small, but attractive. We used chicken wire, tent pegs (for my girl is a master camper, an ingenious builder, a brilliant strategist), an old metal pole as a post, popped into the ground with the sledgehammer fuelled by strong teenaged muscles bronzed by summer sun.

The sheep worried the fence and the chickens got out. The sheep got in. The new pup, Sydney, an Australian shepherd desperate to work, caught the chickens, one by one, and held them down until one or the other of us, called by the indignant squawking of the hens, came and made the release. The chickens were ruffled and somewhat defeathered, but fine.

We needed reinforcements. We dragged extra wooden hurdles over from the stable and pounded in stronger posts. We diverted the sheep to a distant field, and now the chickens are settling in. They're laying again, growing new feathers after their moult, redefining their pecking order. The hobbled chicken is alone in the old pen; she was cannibalized so badly there was a hole the size of a quarter in her back, pooled with blood. I dared not let her out. But she too is better. With the water turned off, the floor is dry. I just give her a drink in an old bread pan, a little feed each day, and now she is back on her lay. Two eggs in the past two days. And feathers have grown on her back, camouflaging, if not healing, the wound. At first they were just quills, like a porcupine's, clear and thick and thorny, but then the shafts grew fuzz on the ends, like the soft edges of fine paper on a closed fan. Now the feathers are like velvet chestnut-coloured scales layering down her back. Rudimentary, but beautiful. She struts, she clucks, she lays. And soon, I hope, she will be able to join her mates, hold her own, find her place and still survive. And soon, I hope, we will clean out her pen, fix the leak and redecorate the winter residence. We'll remove the holland cloths, dust off the pictures, add fresh flowers. The chickens will be able to walk across the barnyard, scratching as they go, and strut into the warm dry land of Cairo for the winter. They will bed down in golden straw ripened by Ra himself.

⤙ *HECTOR* ⤚

⤳ NOW THAT THE DOMESTIC birds are debrogued, debooted, unlaced and running footloose through the long grass, my eyes turn to the wild fowl once again. All started well this year. The bluebirds, who succeeded with a late nesting last summer, arrived together, paired. They scouted, preened, surveyed, tested one box and another, then departed in a storm. It was a late spring, the latest I could ever remember. They retreated for a couple of weeks to warmer winds, where they could forage, rest, exchange billets-doux.

When they returned they seemed dubious of the renovated box, which was stately on its post and subdued in its grey PVC pest-protector. Though nothing was going to shinny up and attack this year's fledglings, the would-be parents were not co-operating. Were not moving in.

Twice I emptied the box of tree swallow bedding. The

invaders, beautiful in their shimmering deep-green Italian suits with stark white shirt fronts, are dive-bombers. They frequently argue about property rights. I am prepared to share; they clearly are not. So I discourage them as neighbours. They build extravagant nests, works of art piled with large feathers like eighteenth-century court chapeaux. Tree swallows are classy in their iridescent formal dress, but a bit overstated, meretricious.

Bluebirds, while breathtakingly beautiful and stunningly bright, balance visual display with a sweet demeanour, a gentle reserve, a commitment to collaboration and communal living. They share. But not with tree swallows. Instead of fighting, my cerulean pair retreated to a distant box on the fencerow, down the sheep lane, past the Alexandrian chicken coop, the drive-shed and the old log house. I checked the box one day, seeing the bluebirds nearby, and found the nest crafted. The next time I looked there were three perfect blue eggs, and the time after that there were five. Birds don't sit until their clutch is complete. The eggs remain dormant until the female begins incubation. Then the eggs develop together. She laid. She sat. They hatched.

I wasn't able to observe as much in this location—which might have been their plan—of the nuance of the courtship, the gestation support, the offerings of bugs and tasty morsels, the recognition of cravings and ravings as they prepared for parenthood. I was vigilant in my concern though, for now they were once again in a perilous situation atop a cedar fence post, which was rough, climbable.

I planned their protection from intruders. My children's outgrown sled, a round plastic saucer in an unnameable neon hue, lay discarded in the drive shed. With my secateurs I cut to the saucer's centre and snipped out a circle. I arranged the garish collar around the post under the box, where it became a plastic ceiling to climbers, slitherers, shinniers. I willed the bluebirds to overlook the aesthetic insult, recognize the thought and stay and raise a family. The collar screamed bad taste, outshone the bursting buds, competed with the lilacs for attention, dwarfed spring flowers, clashed with everything. But the birds stayed, accepted my gaudy assistance and got on with it.

During my ramblings I marked their progress, checked the nest, noted the growth of the nestlings. I always knocked on the door, but the female never flew out the hole; either I timed my checks with her wanderings or she fled when I opened the box, narrowly missing me in her reluctant exit. There were at least four babies, possibly five; I never stayed long enough to be sure.

Just when they were getting big enough to plan their futures, go for their first solo flights, a time when their nutritional needs were demanding, almost constant, the male bluebird discovered an enemy.

Neither cat nor hawk, this foe was of his own image. Leaving his perch in the maple tree, he approached the glass of my loft window, veered away, and approached again. At times he landed on the window frame, sneaked peeks inside from the corner of his eye. Sidelong glances. He puffed out, made himself big and blue and mean. His double did the same. They played at this game, ruffling, sneering, threatening, for most of the morning. If I stood right against the window, he would fly off to the safety of the tree, but as soon as I settled even a short distance away, he was back at it, flopping himself against the glass, menacing his reflection, looking formidable.

Obscure the glass, I thought. He will never see himself through glass darkly. So I taped up curtains made from scraps of fabric, a weaving apron, newspaper. I obliterated the whole window—my well-earned spring light gone—to save him from himself. But to no avail. This bird could see only the outer reflection, and no amount of screening or reasoning would persuade him to call a truce.

Meanwhile his family was outgrowing its home. The baby birds were spilling over the nest, stepping on each other's heads to get the next morsel from their mum. She was frantically catching bugs to feed them. A single mother, left alone to cope on the home front. She had no extended family here, no grandparents or older siblings; she had to feed herself and her babies, watch over them, worry and keep the nest clean all by herself. The fecal sacs came out as fast as the food went in. She was an ornithological taxi providing goods and services around the clock.

The stupidity of the male bluebird's personal war struck me. Pointless, consuming, it caused trauma to himself and others. His participation in the attacks served no purpose but to aggravate us all. I cut the grass under the window, hoping the lawn mower would deter him. But no, it emulated the sound of heavy artillery, of tanks and cannons. He loved it and fought all the harder to eradicate his rival. He played out his strategy until he was blue in the face.

In desperation, I called the conservation authority for advice. I was told to tape black circles of paper to the inside of the glass. The science centre suggested taping a silhouette of a sparrow hawk flying. I tried. I bought black paper. I cut out circles. I cut out sparrow hawks. I taped them to the inside of the glass. He still bashed. He was single-minded. He was bloodthirsty. He wanted to rule the roost. Protect his family. A family that paradoxically was straining to survive without his help. A family that had no rival to fear, no enemy to fight, no bones to pick. They were just getting on with it while his testosterone rose on the wing.

Inside barriers were not helping. Only cutting the reflection would convince him there was nothing to fight about, no territory at risk, no threat to his virility. He had to be stopped from the outside. And this was an upper floor window. And I don't do heights.

My children would have helped. If I had convinced my daughter to hold chickens, miserable creatures to her, surely she would have climbed the house for me. And my son was stretching skyward at an alarming rate, which made climbing less and less necessary to reach almost anything. And Thomas frequently follows my obsessions and fills in for my inadequacies. But no one was around. All were gone, all away. The problem was in my hands alone.

The ladder lay nearby since screen-setting season was in swing. It's not a bad ladder: aluminum extension, light, sturdy, with safe swivel feet to go to ground. I got it up to the roof of the lean-to—plenty of ladder extended above the roofline—and considered my task. There are wires from house to barn. The roofline slopes, though not too much, and the cedar shingles, still with fresh memories of the swamp, are slippery and smooth. I thought of roofers nailing fresh evergreen to ridges for luck. I thought of their jokes about long toenails for gripping. I thought of the carpenter in the halo brace, who had scrambled on my roof like a kid on a climber.

I pondered my ruse. Black circles, a sparrow hawk and an owl silhouette? Or perhaps a scare-bird?

Armed with duct tape, scissors, an old pair of coveralls and a bright blue baseball cap, I mounted the rungs with trepidation. I thought of coroner's cases and broken limbs and the stupidity of taking risks to save a bird from himself. And I continued to mount the rungs.

The window fills the gable end of the loft. Four panels of double glass angle to a peak, a modern Gothic attempt at salvation. But it was heaven I was trying to save the bird from. The first stretch was simple and I reached the roof. I threw the coveralls and hat ahead onto the shingles, tossed the tape on the mass of fabric and checked for the scissors in my pocket. A deep breath and I was over the top, perched. I repressed thoughts of the inevitable trip down.

It was terrifying to tape my effigy to the window. I spread out the arms of the coveralls and duct-taped them to the window frame, fastened the shoulders and the collar and attached the legs in a manner I hoped the bluebird would think was a human form. I saw him watching me as I mounted the hat, and I wondered if he was just waiting for me to leave before resuming his brawl. But when at last I got myself over the edge and down, I could see that he was cautious. He backed off. Went back to the field.

Perhaps bluebirds are like two-year-olds: intent on a project, unrelenting in its pursuit, but distractible. My coveralls succeeded. The bluebird gave up his bashing. He returned to the nest in glory. The battle over, the enemy conquered, the territory retained. He was a hero. There were no dead to carry or bury, no wounds to bind, no enemy to drag in the dust by the heels, just victory.

TWO DAYS LATER he was back and swerving at the glass, menacing his doppelgänger, his nemesis. A storm had loosened the tape; the coveralls were in a heap on the roof, a pile of rags. Virginia Woolf told us that women have served as looking glasses for men, have reflected them back at twice their size. My bird's anger toward an identical self-image was out of control. No wonder women are at such risk. He was violent, riled, ready to fight.

Amused, I got out the staple gun, reassembled the artifice securely to the sash, watched the bird back off and forget. But bliss did not last. To the west, just outside a glass door on the ground, lay a flash of blue. The female. Lifeless, her neck was broken. Had the male warned her of the foe? Did she enlist to protect her young? Or had she merely sailed along in the early light, viewing only clear sky, an open passage, a freeway? The unanswerable. The sorrow of this event. A beautiful, needed creature, dead at my feet.

I checked the box. Empty. Messy, dirty, well-worn and abandoned. I recalled the screech of a hawk at dawn. I feared the worst. The entire family, all but the marauding father, gone.

He stuck around, feeding from perches in the apple trees on the lawn, swooping to catch insects, flying into the maples with mouthfuls of moth, beakfuls of beetle. I heard him *chur wi* and gurgle. Was he feeding heavily, perhaps sharing his catch? There was no evidence of offspring.

Then suddenly they reappeared: four unsteady babies, blue around the edges, specked in front, tottering on the wire in a row. They were out, they were alive, they were being fed. Their father had transformed from pugilist to provider. He was raising his young alone.

A NEW CLUTCH will usually vanish by August. The family stays and feeds for a few weeks after fledging, then retreats from the summer stage. Perhaps the parents go farther north where the bugs are bigger and more plentiful, or perhaps I just don't see them because their feathers fade into camouflage after the breeding season ends.

But this year I caught the odd glimpse of birds on wires at dusk, little colour in the fading light, but unmistakably the soft-shouldered bluebird shape.

I checked the boxes. After its brood of tree swallows, the window box was taken over by the wrens who built right on top of the old nest. They woke me each morning with their chatter. A week ago I cleared the wren twig-fill from the fence rowhouse, a ruse they use to discourage other birds from nesting. Wrens spend hours moving twigs; they've filled my clothespin bag twice.

Something caused me to check the boxes again yesterday. I had been weeding and working, and something compelled me to look. I knocked on the side of the box and waited. Nothing. I pulled the pin which holds it shut and slowly lifted the panel. A nest. Not twigs, but dried grass. Not messy, but well-woven, compact, neat. I lifted further and a small black eye peered at me from a crouched feathered body. Using the holding pin which fastens the door shut, I lowered the edge of the nest to glance at the buried bird. She fled in a flash of blue, revealing three perfect turquoise eggs. A new female. A new brood. Beginning again.

← *CORDUROY ROAD* →

🐦 IF YOU FOLLOW THE LANE beyond the summer chicken run, the drive shed and log house, the fancy-collared bluebird box and the rail gate into the bee yard and carry on down the hill, either turning to the south and walking between the tree line and page-wire fence to the top of the swamp, or straight west through the thicket of cedars and smattering of maples and cherries, you will reach the forest of Lambsquarters. The bush lies at the bottom of the hill. Thick, dense, overgrown and mysterious, it beckons, draws in the eye and begs for the body to follow. Full of riches and undiscovered treasures, it was impassable when we came, undisturbed for years by human footfall, unobserved home to hundreds of species.

MAYBE IT WAS his sense of the pioneer that motivated Thomas to discover the methods of the homesteaders.

Buying an old farm and being in touch with its ancestors through the remains of their log house, the bottle caches wherever we tried to dig a garden, the ancient ropes and pulleys in the barn. Perhaps that, and those early words of wisdom from our faraway friend—that only skills and knowledge are tangible—made Thomas decide to learn pioneer ways. To become a survivor, a maker. A carver of paths and a cutter of roads. Or maybe it was the frustration of hauling firewood out of a forest that was more marsh than highland, his boots sinking and suctioning, mud oozing and squelching. Or possibly he just wanted to open up the bog and let the sun in, the children through, the dogs along. Not that there were children when he began. Not that any of the dogs we've had here needed help. They followed their noses under the brush and through the cedar tangles and deadfalls that make this bush a continuous warren of wild things. Maybe it was the sheer work involved: the cutting and gathering, the navigation, the creation of order from chaos that makes us human.

Most likely, Thomas picked up a branch, cut down a dead tree, made a pile of logs and wondered what to do with the narrow and short ones. He put two down on the ground parallel to each other. And then a third, and then a fourth, and one by one the logs became a road.

MY NEIGHBOUR Harris told me that there are more trees in this farmland now, more forests and wooded bogs, than there have been since it was first cleared well over a hundred years ago. When the settlers arrived and staked their claims, they slashed and burned. They used large pine logs for houses, timber for barns, hemlock planks for siding, cedar for rail fences and posts, maple for floors and furniture, and all of the treetops for firewood. Elms, which survived for a time by adamantly resisting the axe, were brought to their knees by disease. They were skeletons when we arrived here. Great grey masses of broken bodies waiting for the wind to finish them off.

Cleaning up those dead elms got Thomas to the bush. He brought back wheelbarrow-loads of elm to burn. He used the maul to split it, or the neighbour's chainsaw, which left great square chunks of wood that burned all night in the stove if the fire got hot enough to ignite them.

During severe winters, fires in the two woodstoves are essential. So the forest becomes a place of harvest. A place to scavenge and tidy. A place to protect and nurture. When the sheep flock grew bigger and needed the wild grasses of the open swamp for pasture, we had to build a fence to keep them from the wooded bog, from the maze of deadfall and rabbit tracks, the trillium and bloodroot.

The season of the fence clinched the corduroy road. Fencing through the extensive ground tangle and excessive wood waste was arduous: post holes had to be hand-dug between grills of trees, braces had to be built and wire had to be stretched in cramped, muggy mornings drifting from spring to summer. The leaves unfolded with attending shade, but mosquitoes hatched hourly. That fence forced Thomas to look at the ground, be eye to eye with the elements. Develop an affinity.

ORIGINAL SETTLERS, cutting, chopping, slicing with their crosscut saws, laid down the very first roads with felled trees. They followed native paths, portages and trapping lines, made way for horses, wagons, more immigrants. But soon the townships broke into patchwork quilts run through with Roman roads. Straight lines gave way only for deep lakes, stone-faced ridges, festering swamps. With stumps and rocks studding the land, only logs laid like matches in a box could form a base for concessions and sideroads.

Excess trees from land clearing laid edge to edge make a road only visually similar to its cotton namesake: *Corde du roi*. The king's cord is a fabric soft to the touch with a light-reflecting nap. Corduroy roads, although they do play with light through the lace of leaves, have no soft drape. One hard log lies against another and another, forming a continuous curdle of hills and valleys. Early immigrants were legally required to slog together to build these roads, whose ghosts can be seen each spring as the township graders unearth the splintered remains of former forest trees, forced up through the gravel by frost.

I think of the first families when I see those torn logs. Families sitting on open wagons, fiercely holding their children, riding over waves of a road as choppy as the seas they sailed to get here. The pulse as constant as a racing heartbeat. A nursing mother cradling her newborn against full breasts assaulted by each jolt, and children bruising in their pretence of riding ponies, shooting rapids, rolling down terraced hillsides. Some pioneers carried only the clothes on their backs; others had the dubious burden of trunks full of silver and books to protect. In their bumpity journey they were levelled on a classless plane.

The logs that appear during the spring breakup are all that are left of those roads now. Just memento mori to remind us of our connection with the past. And our impending outcome in the future. Occasionally, farmers still build a bit of corduroy in the bush—they fill in low spots for vehicles during logging. Their form is for function and is ragged and imprecise. Not trimmed, not measured, not calculated to please in itself.

Thomas's road is different. It is function and beauty both. Some say function is beauty, but it doesn't always follow. Or lead. Perhaps beauty depends on the nature of the function. And in the case of Thomas's road, the function is nature.

I gather the road just began with the laying of four-foot lengths of log. All the deadfall from a bush idle for many years. Cedars dying or blown over, not knowing yet they were dead. Permanently on tilt or crashed to the forest floor. Dangerous widow-makers, threatening to fall suddenly on the unsuspecting. Balsams, which just seem to grow up to die (like us all), stand at attention until a great wind levels them or they are lovingly laid out. Their final rest as road.

The bush itself has a high part, where maples and hemlock, beech and black cherry grow, even a nannyberry tree, its trunk a straight link to the clouds. The high forest needs no corduroy, is rarely wet, is always accessible. But it leads off to lower ground directly. To the swamp cedar and the aspen, the poplar and the thick underbrush and bulrush. There are beauties in a bog, but access is the problem. How do you tramp through the terrain when you sink with each step? You don't. Unless, of course, you have corduroy to step on.

Thomas has taken years to thread his road through the acreage. It winds and meanders and connects with the two ends on high ground. It has absorbed every dead tree that has fallen. It's a conservationist's road. A road that makes life from death. A coroner's road.

Like some magic lens turned around corners, like fibre optics, the road opens up the inaccessible. The secrets of the marsh are revealed. Suddenly we can walk on water. We can walk the bog. Each season spreads itself across the landscape on either side of the narrow winding path.

Winter landscape passes quickly on skis. The mushrooms of snow on stumps; the cattails of snow on bul-
rushes already bursting with their own internal cotton
wool. The black eye of a snowshoe hare perfectly camouflaged against his white world. In winter the views are
quick and crisp. Sleeping nature.

Spring awakens with the thaw. Before bugs or
leaves, the forest yawns awake. Sap runs. Small shoots
of horsetail—prehistoric plant, brown, speckled black,
alien—push ancient genes through spaces in the road.
Bullfrogs croak, peepers peep. Warblers in bare trees
sing, flash yellows and blues, reds and blacks on
the starkscape. Ruffed grouse drum. Water burbles the
edges, mud oozes, but the road holds, carries us into
this heart of marshness.

Slowly, green arrives. And the road leads to details.
The minutiae of life on the edge. Iris poke through the
marsh with the promise of blue and yellow flags. Rigid
horsetails morph to fine feathers, yellow-green and soft.
Trilliums, red and white, and bloodroot grow on higher
ground. The showy but shy flower of the ground ginger
hides under leaf mould. The canopy begins overhead,
budding, then unfurling into dappled skies, filtering sun
and rain both. This stage is quick in Grey County, where
spring can last just days before a heat wave arouses everything through to an orgasm of greens and abundance.
There's so much to see, but blackflies and mosquitoes,
fighting for territory and ownership, rush the body

through the bush. Orchids, tiny pink salacious snake-mouths. And mushrooms. And morels.

Then full summer days begin with marsh marigolds massing, drifting into iris and angelica, soaring their arrowhead buds into the ether and opening as cumulus clouds of bloom. Lobelias begin—first the red *cardinalis*, then later the blue *siphilitica*—and spotted jewel-weed spreads tender stems under the cedars. Nettles encroach a spot: if you have bare legs stay to the middle. Time passes. Fireflies strobe. Cicadas hum like errant wires.

August is a time of thick dews. Spiderwebs of gold and silver cross the road and are rebuilt each night by Penelope and Arachne working their own secret fates. Goldenrod, Joe-pye weed and fleabane, fall aster and touch-me-not. Things are going to seed. Iris pod like little peppers. Ragweed at large in the air.

Then a sudden frost. The first red leaf. A next and a next. Gold and brown and orange. The forest begins to die. It does not go gentle.

As the road circles through the bush, so the season follows—or leads. The man I live with has opened up the way, has revealed the secrets of the swamp. But only to those who will look, who will slow to the speed of the snail to see, who will suffer the slings of blackflies and the arrows of nettles to experience outrageous fortune. He lets me walk on water.

✦ *TROWEL* ✦

THE FOREST TOOLS ARE LARGE, sharp, wicked: bucksaws and swede saws, axes and hatchets, and chainsaws, which pollute with noise, the odour of fuel, and require the armour of Kevlar and steel. The tools travel in the wheelbarrow or trailer, which is hitched to the Ford or the baby John Deere. Or they dangle from Thomas's long arm in an old white pail, quixotically labelled "leaks fluids" as if dreams could be held there intact, or solid plans or ideas. He can swing the saw over one shoulder and hold the axe by its neck, but usually he has more to carry than that. So he dons his overalls or his chaps or both and is panoplied for his fray with woods that are ever encroaching on the waterward road, ever falling and felling, responding to the vagaries of the elements.

He heads down the thinning fall meadow, through the late grazing flock, around the centre stone-pile and shade

cedars and disappears through the gate, over the swamp
edge and into the forest, past the stumped area we call
Knock-down Corner and beyond into the Bush and away.
And while he trudges and trims, piles and stacks, orders
the deadfall into posts and lumber, kindling and road fill,
I garden unarmed near home. I harvest or deadhead,
divide or weed. My tools are manageable in my hands, tiny,
efficient and light. I almost always use a trowel.

A trowel is a double-edged sword. A hand tool with
a thin, flat double blade for mortaring rock or plastering walls, or a small, scooped shovel for opening the
earth to receive or relinquish young plants. The word
derives from the Latin *trua*, meaning "ladle," or *trulla*,
meaning "spoon." In its way the trowel does provide
nourishment to those who pick it up. It feeds an aesthetic need and reinforces the power of production. It
feeds the simple pleasure inherent in the skill to build
or grow.

Trowels are strong symbols for Lambsquarters. With
them we throw mortar, plant seedlings, smooth plaster,
weed and thin. Trowels were among the first tools here,
and they remain crucial to the farm.

The house saw few changes in its first hundred
years. Rudimentary electricity at mid-century led to
pumped water and primitive indoor plumbing. A telephone. A Romanesque archway that must have grown
from a simple doorway between the front and back
parlours, small rooms both, joined now by a vaulted

entrance, the only curve in a structure of strict straight lines. Paired sconces graced this graceless passage, a token of frivolity surrounded by austerity. This aberrant arc, which neither separated nor joined the cramped little rooms, had to go. We attacked the plaster with the wrecking bar, pried out the lath, dismantled the studs and found ourselves (when the dust settled) with a large bright room, punctuated with a branch line of void in the wall. I bought a trowel.

I'd never plastered before, but Lionel, the building-store man, who had taken on the cause of the renovation, assured me it was simple. He sold me a huge bag of plaster and the trowel and gave mixing instructions. So there I was, hod in hand, my first batch of mud ready to throw, my shiny pointed trowel securely nestled in my fist, its wooden handle warm in a room still awaiting central heat. It was January.

Before buying the plaster trowel, I had invested in the cheapest of garden trowels the previous fall. We bought the farm in October, and having no way of knowing what might appear in the derelict gardens the following spring, I planted as many daffodils as I could around the apple trees in the front orchard. The trowel was an inferior one. It immediately became acquainted with the rock population just under the surface of the ground and succumbed. It was the first of many.

By the time I got to plastering, I'd already mastered

the arts of demolition, wood splitting and stove starting, fuse replacing, wallpaper stripping, lino lifting and dump going. I thought I could do anything. I liked the feel of the trowel. I loved the feel of the throw. Plaster mixed perfectly careens off the blade and sticks exactly where it's sent. Catch for one player, and never a miss. The throw comes off the topside, after scooping with one blade, but the bottom is the spreader, its pointed end directing morsels of muck into corners, angling one side to eke out the fill to the other edge, smoothing along the original wall to make a perfect join. Artistry and play and serious work in one action, like Ceramus's pottery.

It took a day to fill both walls, to mix and pitch and level, and to stand back and admire this pristine stripe, white against the grungy grey of the old plaster that had been papered so many times without ever seeing the light. Papered and papered and painted over to obscure any whisper from the ghosts of the original plasterers.

My trowel got little rest after its initiation. Jack posts in the basement raised the centre of the house about the height of a hand, cracking the walls above the doors, leaving huge gaping holes and piles of plaster on the floor. Mouse holes (arches I thought existed only in cartoons) appeared under the layers of pasted wallpaper, and more than once my trowel's work was defeated next day by squatter's rights.

By spring I was trowelling outside, pointing stone foundations and bricks, and digging in earth rich in nutrients, ready for flowers and fruits. The stonework was haphazard, required a different kind of muck, and the bricks have a trowel of their own, a narrow pen-sized instrument, curved to snug the space between the rows, ooze out the excess and cut it off with an edge. Small beer.

I have had countless garden trowels, cheap metal objects, painted white or green or yellow, with plastic or wooden handles, wide blades or narrow. For years I replaced them as I ruined them, Some succumbed at first thrust, first tilt. Trowels are not levers. I tried plastic blades (they don't penetrate), soft handles (they bend), narrow shafts (they collapse). Then I bought the perfect trowel. It was forged steel, expensive, strong, trusty. Its blade was slim but not anorexic; its handle solid but not rough. It was my twin all spring: where I went in the garden, it came too.

During the long days of spring, starting right after morning chores when the sun rises early and the dew sinks into thirsty ground, I follow the dandelion roots down to their underworld, passing the three-headed Cerberus of dog bur, dogbane and dog grass. The dog bur is the best. It's sticky and prickly but has an easy root to lift. Dog bane is woody and puts up a tough resistance. Dog grass is the worst. Its roots weave an impenetrable and unending subterranean labyrinth. A Heraclean task.

Morning weeding and afternoon planting. When the sun is soft and the earth warm, my trowel makes the hole, mounding earth aside. I water, place and plant, tamp with the back of the blade, scoop the fresh soil in place, move to the next. Pungent basil, reeking tomatoes, and hot peppers, which dare me to touch my face, the trowel settles them all in their rows. Distant neighbours who will grow into intimate friends.

By evening, when the blackflies swarm and the light wanes, I take my pail, my pots, my trowel to the tap and rinse and park them for another day.

One morning, my perfect trowel was gone. Vanished. Thomas had been mortaring by the tap. He'd put in a new window well, moved rocks back, dug a trench, poured cement, smoothed, flattened with his mason's tool, mortared new rock sides into place with skill. The job had taken weeks and had somehow swallowed my trowel. Trowelled it in. Like a time capsule, or an interment, or a pomegranate mistakenly eaten. It was gone, never to surface again with no one to bargain for its release. I've never found another like it.

THE STONE TROWELS are never idle in season. Their work began with Grant Mather, a stonemason with long hair and a penchant for Earl Grey tea. He laboured one summer on the barn courtyard, rebuilding a wall that something didn't love. Rubble and promise, remnants of its former life as foundation, the stones and mortar lay in ruin, cannoned, crumbled, humbled and low. And Grant, who but for an *i* and an *e* would be the rock itself, spread his tools amongst the wildflowers (*Mather* meaning "camomile") and slowly brought the wall back from death. He split, he placed, he eyed and he smoked. He butted his joints in the mortar and carefully sealed their tombs. He taught me to mix, to point and to place. He taught Thomas to split, to lift, to design. He taught us the physics and the aesthetics. And, oh, the trowels! Tiny mortaring trowel babies, spoon-sized, butter-knifed. Large capacious trowels, hungry for the hod. Grant spread his perfect mix and the stones grew from rubble into a mural of pinks and greys, purples and greens.

I followed his teaching, learned my lessons, took my wheelbarrow to the sand pile, shovelled in the mix, added water in small amounts. Too little water makes the mortar grainy, dry and unmanageable; too much and you have a slurry. Mortar should feel like snow on the shovel. The trowel cuts down and lifts, forms a liquid edge around a tight pack of muck. It comes off the forehand like a shuttlecock, sails through the air with a flick of the wrist and lands in the crevice, a perfect score.

The following summer was mine. I had my own sand pile, my own trowel, a whole barn foundation to point, inside and out. The bank side is underground, but inside is a solid rock face, stones outlined with the empty holes and spaces of mortar past. On the hottest days, the stones were cool. Sheltered from the sun, wedged against the dark earth to the north, they waited calmly with a cold dignity to be redefined, reglued, renewed with fresh mortar, with the gentle stroke of the trowel. I hosed them down, flushed out the crumbling bits of cement and straw, the grains of sand and dirt, and began my pitch and throw. I got in a few back-hands and side-swipes, and mastered the art of the tool. The west wall with outside exposure I saved for early fall, when the sun was low and less intense and warmed my back in the afternoons. I worked in patches, mortaring deep, returning to point, then back once again to fin-ish the smooth edge, determined that no crevice would be left to hold water, allow frost to enter, or crack and attack the wall, sending it tumbling to Frost's condition.

The west wall extends into the barnyard, evidence of the original bigger barn. It sloped with decay, its outer edge eroded to one big situpon rock. I repaired the wall gently, leaving the slope, filling the holes, cap-ping the top. But one summer the mature John Deere tractor, steered by the youngest Harris son, connected the manure spreader with the wall and the spreader won. It cracked the mortar and loosened the rock. The situpon, also used as a mountain path by agile lambs, became treacherous.

Grant was gone by now—moved to a rockier rid-ing—and I called another mason to help. He never came. So one day Thomas eyed the rubble, decried the danger, took up the trowel and began the repair. He revelled in the combination of brute strength, physics, geometry and artistry required to build with stone. He gathered special specimens, chose them for their colour, texture and tone, and brought them from distant parts of the farm. He hauled rocks high into the air with hands he hadn't known he had. And too soon the wall was finished.

By fall he'd found a new venue: the bottom of the Sidefield, more than two rods long. He commenced to dig and gather material for a roadside stone fence. Rock piles everywhere were in danger of depletion; favourite stones, jumping and stepping stones disappeared and were replaced with fresh earth and small seedlings of trefoil. Magic stones, monster stones, round rocks and mound rocks seemingly grew legs and took themselves to the site, nestled in to wait for placement, hoped for an outside spot, gave up their moss.

The foundation hole was so big it took a ready-mix truck to fill it. This was to be a serious wall. Levels and plumb lines, stone splitters and hammers, steel-toed boots and crowbars appeared at the scene, and after the first course was placed, out came the mortar and trowel.

The wall grew on two sides and two ends. The middle was a dump for rubble rocks, rejects in size, those bits that broke off in the glacier, got rounded in the crush. They were gathered by the barrowful, tipped into the goo and trowelled in, globful after globful, sounding *thunk* as they went. Not beautiful, these rocks, settled in between the glorious carapace of granite and limestone, conglomerate and quartz, but they formed a solid skeleton nevertheless, the backbone of the wall, hidden, veiled, but vertebral in strength and substance.

The wall rose in courses, rows of rocks that were chosen to harmonize with their neighbours, not just to east and west, but also above and below. And it was slow, cerebral work. Much of the planning weighed as Thomas leaned on the end of the crowbar. He took careful measure of mass and force, surface and density, shade and hue. The gargantuan rocks were moved with magic, with faith, with smoke and mirrors, with the help of our son, now solid himself and tall and strong and capable of shifting great weights. With the crowbar, some boards, the wheelbarrow, and the brilliant use of an old wooden ladder, propped on the morphing structure to convey massive boulders up, against gravity, a rung at a time. Higher and higher the wall grew. Mortar disappeared as fast as snow in May, was swallowed by the wall like rain by parched earth slaking its thirst. And always the trowel flicked, filled, flattened, tamped and trimmed until the summit was attained and the mortar cap went on. From mounded top to flat bottom, the trowel stamped the wall as done, curbed its growth and sealed its fate.

Thomas had another mentor mason, a neighbour up the road. He was a philosopher by profession, a painter by talent and a stone builder by inclination. He created the most whimsical of structures. He made a garden wall that is full of holes, and a pentagonal secular abbey with local rock, broken tombstones and antique carved lintels. He niched the two-storey abbey with treasures and filled it with art. His *pigeonnier*, constructed on stone stilts, supports a sculptured blend of a bird in flight and a fish. Beaked in front and fan-tailed behind, it swims in a cerulean wooden frame painted to blend with the sky. He taught Thomas how to scavenge for stone. He taught patience and colour and form. His counsel was firm, his praise was scant and his opinion is now just a memory, for he died too soon. The medieval alchemists would be astonished to see what he created. The fabled philosopher's stone, which turns all base metals into gold, was his secret. But he was not a secretive man, and he shared his skills. Stone creations sprouted all over the township under his tutelage. One of them is Thomas's wall at the bottom of our lane.

ONE LATE FALL DAY I went to the wall, which was not yet finished, but put away for the season, and saw rust on the rock. It had been bloodied when a boulder had dropped on Thomas's hand, splitting his finger like a sausage. Blood had filled my own fair mason's glove and had spilled onto his boots and his art, his creation of unyielding stone. He stormed into the house unable to speak, unable to look at the damage he had done, unable to feel the pain of the crush or to reconcile the danger. Our daughter, grown and calm and competent, had taken over the kitchen to cook the meal, a celebratory dinner turned meaningless as I drove Thomas at speed to town where the young medic soothed his pain as she stitched him together, saved his face and his hand.

Now, seeing the remnant of his life's blood still on the rock, I decided to pay homage to this wall, this shell of a wall-to-be. I secretly fetched my garden trowel and a basket full of bulbs. Spreading the leaves, I dug on both sides of the wall and dropped scilla, grape hyacinth and crocus roadward, and daffodils, which the sheep won't eat, on the field side. Carefully replacing the leaves with my trowel, I mused on the mixture of mortar and earth, blood and sweat, the meeting of trowels at this structure. It rises now as a measure of the solidity of this place. I planted my bulbs as a sacrifice to its stature and as an offering to its builder.

This is the sublime: the simplicity of the tools and the intensity of their creations.

⤙ *STILES* ⤚

🪶 WALLS AND FENCES, boundaries and barriers keep things in. And out. They form aesthetic lines, staffs of meandering music in cedar rails or solid rock foundations in the stones of our land. Fences suggest entry by invitation only. Unless, of course, you are a bird or a seed wafting over, a snake slithering through, or a blade of grass rooting sideways to the other side. The stone fence is bordered by a gate into the Sidefield, is amenable to climbing, sitting and walking. It harbours sempervivum, lichen and the promise of vine.

Elsewhere on the farm the boundary fences contain. There are no gates for egress, for escape. The fences form solid penning, connecting and dividing neighbours. They haven't always held. The pig who arrived at the back door on Easter Sunday, snuffling and snorting and frightening me before I figured out who it could be, had rooted her way round the rails edging the swamp, crashed one down, lifted another and followed the path to the house. The Easter pig.

Cattle broke through the wire into the Hayfield, ate some of the crop and trampled more. A Jersey bull set up camp on the front lawn for a whole spring day before I could discover who owned it. Goats sail over the top of any kind of fence, are not containable and are not missed. And occasionally a few of my sheep have gone astray through a weak fence and grazed their way to the neighbour's grass.

In winter every fence has its up point, its area prone to snow, which fills in until the posts are gone, the rails buried and the fence a mere memory of pales past. Skis fly over top with nothing to stop them; the property goes on forever. But by spring, when the ground is firming up, the rails lean forward through tangle and brush, angling awkwardly over and down, and the climb becomes difficult. The kids never complained. My daughter was always an expert scrambler; my son grew so tall he could almost step over. But I begged for a stile, cajoled for a stile, and finally, when the woods-man felled the dead elm on the fencerow, I took short lengths of log, arranged them on both sides of the rail, slipped a board through and I had a way across. It was wobbly and primitive, but it was a step. This motivated Thomas and he arrived with his saw, his sense of order and form and improvement. He tinkered with my mess and turned it into something beautiful and steady and safe. A mirror of himself: a solid stile to help me over any barrier, face any obstruction and get to the land beyond it.

Once he understood about stiles, he took them on. Particularly when he realized he could make them with rock.

All along the inside of the meadow fence is garden. It has grown, over the years, spread from the few perennials that survived the plough, the bachelors and the neglect, into a border that runs from barnyard to road. The garden weaves in and out of the lawn, through the groves of lilacs and cedars, the shade of maples and the worrying noses of browsing sheep on the other side. There is one gate into the field by the house, but it serves neither back nor front gardens well. Though it is rail, the fence is not good for climbing as I've discreetly lined it with wire netting that I renew and repair each spring to deter ovine marauders. The rails refuse a foothold.

Rocks have been my rescue. A huge boulder, moved by magic or memory, stands on end in the field, high enough for one big step over the top. On the garden side, amidst short spreading lamium, there are flat flags leading to the stepping stone that boosts me over. Nothing tall grows here but the rock—just short plants the sheep can't reach through the open space I've left beside the stile so Sydney the dog has her own path. She runs at speed, turning sideways at the last moment, and just like Zoë before her, flies through the fence to land with a twist. We can be in the field in a second if we spot a problem or take a whim.

To the south, amidst the blue garden, there is another path of rocks, flat to begin with, then mounding to the lift over the fence, letting me through to another trail to the field. It leads me to harvest the pears, and to prune them against their constant determination to grow up rather than out. It leads me to the locust trees and sumac at the roadside, the escapes of *Tulipa tarda* and scilla, grape hyacinth and narcissus, which I dig out with my trowel and transplant on the tame side of the fence. Harnessed back into my garden, they only seem to grow to escape once more.

Stiles take me out and bring me back. They are two-way streets that open up my land and return me to its heart. They provide the possibility of a walk most days until the snow whitewashes them away.

↞ *STORM-STAYED* ↠

SOMETIMES THERE IS WARNING for our legendary snowstorms, which fill all hollows, mound all hills. We've learned over the years to read skyscapes: the mare's tails and mackerel scales in the clouds, the black northern horizons, the grey streamers fronting in from the west, which herald the steady march of the lake-effect troops. Sometimes the news alerts us to the upcoming squalls. The radio interruptions and General Store gossip in Alderney, the flurry of activity as everyone rushes to the village for supplies while the getting's good. Canned foods, milk, animal feed. Fresh vegetables and fruit and extra treats for kids who might be stranded at home ravenous from snow play or shovelling. We get a full tank of fuel in the car, bring firewood in from the fencerow and, if the power's threatened, store water in the tub, for electricity runs the pump from the well.

It's a Grey County expression, to be storm-stayed.
It differs from being snowed in or snowbound, which
suggest hot drinks and warm fires within safe walls.
Being storm-stayed is serious business in the snowbelt.
It can happen in your car, in town if the roads are
closed by the police, at home, or anywhere else you
might be when the storm hits.

The news is full of ominous reports of an
approaching storm: squalls, streamers, blizzards and
hazards. But it's already midday; Thomas left for work
long ago without a change of clothes, without a thought
that he might be stuck in town for days.

By the time the school bus returns, the first flakes
are falling. My grown children walk up the lane, stepping over the drifting dunes of snow while gusts gather
in the east. The beast. Aeolus, warden of the winds,
raises his gale slowly at first till it swirls and tangles,
chills and bites. The snow fingers become full-bodied
drifts, hills and valleys rising from the flat desert on the
once sandy lane.

My son shovels out the garage then closes it, lowers
doors, checks latches, battens down hatches while my
daughter and I take the dog to herd the flock into the
barn. Their winter fleece is iced pure white; the black
sheep is in disguise, in white-face for the day. We shut
them in first with a panel then dig the frozen fodder,
bedding, manure and snow that fills the threshold,
obscures the channel for the massive door, its track

high up, valanced, protected. We dig with fork, spade and crowbar, slide the door to, stay the wind from.

After dark the winds explode, volleying white snow off black skies. Eddies and currents pattern the air, dervishing snow into drifts to the tops of fences, to the bottoms of windows set well above ground. Stiles lie buried until spring.

Thomas is stuck in Murphy's Mill, tense in the knowledge that he is alone on call. The roads are closed to evacuation. I wake often in the night, alone in my bed, cold and agitated with the howling of the blizzard, the weight of the snow, fret for all the creatures I care for here. Responsible.

Dark morning is marbled with the smoke of squalling snow. The Jubilee radio station announces local bus cancellations to the ironic ostinato of "Get up in the morning get on the bus," but there's a phone chain too. Buses are cancelled. No school. Pass it on.

Heading out, bundled in my barncoat over a down vest, earflaps snug under my hood, sheepskin mitts and high boots on, I can see that the east garage doors will never open and that I must go out the north way where the path is blown free of snow. The dog doors are clear: two raised panels carved out of the larger door and loose but for top hinges. One door swings in, one door swings out. Sydney paws at her out door gingerly, giving me a woeful look after her night inside. I follow, snowshoes in hand, and find a patch of windswept

ground where I can strap them on. I'm equipped now,
as I hadn't been that first year when the snow came up
over my hips and each step was a heroic measure of my
dedication to this life.

I settle into the giant teardrops of wood and gut
and leather and let them carry me across the top of all
the mountains and valleys that miraculously exalt my
once gentle barnyard. Even if the gates were not down,
removed for winter access, they would no longer
impede my way—the drifts are that high. Only the tops
of the fence posts remain as wedged markers in this new
terrain, this sea of white that waves and breaks and continually reconfigures around me.

The lower half of the stable door to the feed room
is buried in snow. It opens out, so I cannot budge it. I
consider returning to the house for a shovel, or using
one of my snowshoes to rabbit my way through to the
feed room. I'm flummoxed by the tenacity and intensity and sheer volume of this falling manna. Then the
brilliance of the Dutch door illuminates my mind. The
door is not just for admitting summer breezes into the
stable, for leaning on when gazing out between hayloads, for hose or cord conduit, for conversation with
my Dutch-born neighbour. No, the door, evident in
sixteenth-century oils where it spills light into interior
spaces like liquid gold, is suddenly my ingress, my
access. The bottom section latches with a hook and eye
on the stable side, but the top—wide tongue-and-

groove boards hewn in another century—has a toggle latch, a curved metal handle on the outside, a bar and catch within. I lift; it rises and the top of the door pulls out and around, rests against the barn wall, held fast in the wind god's open palm. I take off the snowshoes, hoist up, over, drop down and I'm in!

Frontenac and Lanark, my fall kittens, now half-grown cats, mew and burr with excited trills as the snow and I spill into their demesne. The sheep salivate for their breakfast, the chickens cluck and the rooster struts. He's far past his morning crow and ruffled at my delay. I feed out, check resources and observe that waterlines flow, doors enclose, roofs imbricate. I hope the thick layer of snow that has blown through the barn cracks onto the hay and straw in the mows will insulate rather than melt and ferment my forage and sour my fodder. I mentally check through the beasts and tasks and shut the lights. But the door is much higher from the inside, and is hard to mount. There are shovels in here: my crusty square blade with the bentwood handle, a spade, the long flat scoop I use to gather sheep pellets from the cemented barnyard in summer. But I need to get *out* to dig, and the wind is wild and the snow continues to fall in pages, in books.

Back in the stable I find an apple box. A square wooden structure with a flat top, it's the perfect height for picking low branches in fall or climbing through the top of a standard Dutch door in the depths of winter. It boosts my trip over and out and onto the snowshoes again. I dig in my toes, navigate an about-face, latch the top half of the door and head house-ward, secure in the knowledge that the flock is fed and cosy and the storm is outside their day.

All week I snowshoe to the barn every morning and every night—even after the roads are open and the lane is clear and the kids are back at school. It takes that long to blow out the barnyard to the point where I can take my shovel and carve a path to the Dutch door. The fly-ing Dutchman brings the tractor, the snowblower, and carves tunnels through the drifts after the wind abates. He once told me that they don't have Dutch doors in his part of Holland. And I'm sure they don't need them for weather. But they weren't wrong, the old mas-ters. And nothing reflects light like snow.

⤙ *SHEEP PATHS* ⤚

To follow like sheep.
As if mindless.
Thoughtless.
Stupid.

🖋 SHEEP FOLLOW IN AN AGE-OLD pattern of order. Like Sydney, who takes after me through the stile, they trust their leader. Sometimes too well. It's a trust both exploited and denigrated, encouraged and denounced, but singular. When the alpha sheep sets off down a path, the others are sure to rattle their dags behind. But you do have to get the leader going. She alternately heeds the siren's call and fears the terrors of innocent barriers: the Scylla of a misplaced stone, the Charybdis of a shadow. My first few sheep were pets, all named. But they didn't readily learn to come when I called. They followed their dreams, but with no discernment between the gates of ivory, the gates of horn.

In the first cold snap of the first sheep-autumn at Lambsquarters, before the barn rebuilding, before the arrival of the sheep-herding dog, I carved a beast hole in the stable, which looked like an oversized urban cat-door, covered with a sheet of sacking, to woolgather and wind-hinder. Though the sheep could only bene-fit from this come-and-go door, they suspected some-thing on the other side of the small straw-bound threshold. Circe's spell? Neither fresh hay nor warm shelter could entice them to cross the threshold. The door was new, unknown, untried; they would not risk being turned into swine.

I zigzagged behind the mob, small as it was, snap-ping my fingers and clapping my hands. They clustered, flocked, moved forward then broke free, scattering right and left, winnowing in the formation of some ancient country dance. But they did not go in. Would not. Their eyes widened, their nostrils opened in fear at the approach, and they split into two concentric patterns away. We cycled and cycled until, in frustration, I finally remembered that sheep follow. Cream rises: sheep follow. So down I got on all fours in the barnyard. I eyed the flock over my shoulder, created the track and took myself through the door. They were there behind me, all in a line, calm, noble, trusting. They formed their winter path. And I learned that day to lead.

JUST BEFORE the January thaw there are no sheep paths at all, except for the pacing-trail in the pen and the line scuffed away at the base of the mangers, which exposes the dry, hard, frozen manure pack. On the coldest storm days, when the bitter east wind attacks through the updated sliding door, which is left open the width of two pregnant sheep in wool, there are no tracks at all. Just a huddle of beasts, frosted white on cream fleece, white on white, winter white. On those days the frost itself makes tracks, outlining whiskers otherwise unseen, frosting catfish mouths. The sheep look like kittens who've been sniffing in flour tins, with sparkles.

To close them in and out of the weather on such days, I create a path for the track door, which after all the snow and ice cannot find its channel and slide. The sheep watch with worry as I attack the frozen mass of straw, manure and snow. It isn't easy work, and it isn't quiet, and it certainly isn't warm. I dress in typical *bonhomme* fashion, in long johns, jeans, wool socks, sweater, scarf, mitts and toque. I don the snowsuit my father-in-law left behind from a thinner time and felt-lined boots. And I begin to shovel and to chip. The crowbar, its weight lifted and dropped, asks gravity to make a breakthrough. Slowly, a bit at a time, the debris comes away and a trench forms. The axe would work faster, or the heavy maul, but I'd need steel-toed boots and they aren't warm. So I play it safe and struggle on. The sheep disappear behind me in a steam bath of mutton-breath. The spade lifts out the pellets of frozen dung, the chopped bits of straw, the cubes of ice. Somehow there is never much loose snow. In strong winds it travels, fills up the stable far beyond the door, swirls up the walls over inside stones and through the boards high in the mow, salting the stacked hay as if to preserve it from rot.

If sheep leave few tracks in the storm, the mammals in the mow redeem them. Cats, their claws pulled in, use furry mittens with pink suede palms to mark the snow, and the sharp skeletal marks of rodent feet run just ahead of their tracks at a clip. The chase is circuitous and confusing to decipher, tracks sashay and shuttle in the macabre dance of cat and mouse.

In the stable the sheep huddle for warmth, wear a circle in their bedding, and punctuate it with the deep commas of naps in the straw. They pace eventually, more bored than cold, and yearn to follow, to move in a line. When the wind stops, I dig once more in new snow, haul the door along its groove and watch as cooped critters try to bound through, three at a time. They wedge themselves in the doorway until one gives up and retreats, and they fall into their famous follow formation. As they make new tracks in deep snow, I fill the channel with straw, cover it with a board and wedge it tight with the door. The digging will be easier next time. I'll fork instead of pry.

Before the white deluge, they had their path to the Sidefield, their tracks to the apple trees, where late fruit still fell on shallow snow, and grass could be uncovered with the scrape of a hoof. They filed one by one, through a narrow passage between garden and gate, then fanned through the field on the worn gullies of previous Gullivers.

At dusk on those days the order dissolved and mayhem reigned in a moment of remembered lambdom. Heels kicked, heads bunted and all the gambolling of youth condensed into a few minutes of late light. They ran in; they ran out. They led; they chased. Imbedded tracks dissolved in the dark, making the field a mass of jumping wool, which moved like wheat in the wind. You had to be quick to catch it. Like glimpsing the kneeling oxen on Christmas Eve.

Winter trails are limited, hindered by snow and cold. A good storm will fill the barnyard, bury the feeders, block the gates. The adventurous can step over fences on white walkways, wander to the fields beyond and be gone. But nothing beckons from the blue-white wilderness, so the sheep stay, stalk circles and lines from feeder to straw, from shelter to sun, back and forth on the slippery board over the threshold. They click or stomp or jump right through, leaving neat hoofmarks in a narrow swath.

SHEEP LAMB behind closed doors. They make their labour track in a corner, dig a nest with a forefoot, walking back and forth in the timeless distaff pacing of early contractions. Afterwards they follow me as I lead carrying their newborns to a special pen, where tracks are impossible to lay.

On the first day of spring, when the doors open to the light, they rush to be first to the path, the familiar route to fresh green heaven. They run in full-footed jumping gambols, in sideways kicks, in neck-turning tumbles. All the pent-up energy of winter gestation, labour, birth and nurturing explodes in a May Day festival under the sky. They head down the chute between the Meadow and the Hayfield, nibbling and bleating, putting fresh prints in muddy paths silted over in the thaw—and forget their lambs.

Little lamblings look out big new doors framing brave new worlds. Timidly they take a step in the sun, the way you would dip a toe in a lake, then withdraw and run back inside. But their mothers are gone. The lambs bleat and cry. They circle and pace, and just when they are about to give up, their dams come rushing back, all noise and push and bad manners, and claim them before heading out again, *en famille*, to pasture.

Along the chute the track is wobbly, evidence of some secret navigational device wrapped in wool. Like the hound following the scent of a rabbit, the flock undulates along determined lines, hillside or valley-wise, further wearing the path that was worn over and over by their ancestors. They disappear through cedars that grow too close to the ground for me to pursue, and emerge on two roads, the high and the low, to converge on the grass at random. They eat and walk without restraint. No beadles keep them to the path.

They sidle up to the edge of the Pie-shaped Field, trim the cedar woods to a hedge-on-sticks, graze and browse their way. They disappear through the woods, leaving pellets behind, not breadcrumbs, to mark their trail. Single file. A woollen crocodile on the move.

On hillsides they flock to the verge like Pre-Raphaelite sheep, straying and napping or bunting their buddies, oblivious to the danger of Gabriel Oak's young dog, poised to chase them over the brink. Or they worry the fence to the Hayfield, trying to break a new trail to the fresh alfalfa. There they would gorge and bloat until, like more Hardy sheep, they would suffocate unless the trocar could be found in time to pierce their sides and expel the noxious gasses that would build from the unaccustomed fresh forage after a winter of dry feed.

One spring, Belinda, a beautiful Hampshire yearling, ran off, manoeuvred her head through the fence and ate her fill of alfalfa. By the time I found her she had doubled her size and was gasping her last. The gas had formed, the rumen was distended, the diaphragm was trapped, the ewe was dead. What nurtures, also poisons. Eating alfalfa is a matter of moisture and timing. And the balance tips turvy as well: grass wants height before the sheep arrive. Their bottom teeth drag low and damage the early crop.

Sheep teeth are a surprise to some. On the roof of its mouth, a sheep has only an empty hard palate with no teeth at all in front, just a tough cutting board to scrape the grass against. The lower incisors sever it, and the back opposing molars chew it and chew it again. All that grass goes through all these stomachs: the rumen, the reticulum, the omasom and the abomasum. Rumen, reticulum, omasom, abomasum. Like a Latin chant. Euphonic. The sheep chew to the chant's rhythm, marking 4/4 time.

They spend the season following paths and patterns. Out early for dawn grazing and back to the barnyard for a morning nap. Out again mid-morning, then resting in the afternoon shade by the drive shed or cedar copse. The cycle continues through until dusk, when again they return in a line, the alpha sheep in the lead, to the barnyard's safety. Their ongoing odyssey— white threads spread over the loom of the land, then woven up at night, into a tight weft of woollen tufts. The sheep lie ruminating together, their lambs at their sides, stretched out in the comfort of home. Just before dawn the web is picked apart once more, to wander free in rows unravelled along paths the sheep work, back and forth, like shuttles, for another day.

⚹ *TRACKS* ⚹

MY PATH TO THE BARN CHANGES every day. In summer I meander, detour past the roses or through the honeysuckle. In fall, I kick and crunch amidst coloured leaves, and in winter I tread through snow as the wind blows the lane in and the neighbour blows it out. He knows my timing by my tracks, and however hard I try to beat him, there are days when he's here before I've fed my flock. Although he's never said, I feel his slight censure, feel my faint failure, and I resolve to rise earlier the next day, get on task, trudge my track through that fresh frost and do my chores on time.

Country tracks prescribe time-worn expressions: As the crow flies. Shortest distance from A to B. From here to there. Paths, lanes, highways. Sidewalks, ditches, verges. For every mile of road on the way home, there are two of ditch. Corduroy, gravel, macadam. Grey, beige, black. Bumpity, dusty, slick. Our tracks. Slashed through the country like ancient roads carved with uncurved blades, imperialistic impositions on a landscape that undulates, veers and vectors, jags and juts, resisting straight lines. If we measured crows with our instruments, would they fly straight?

Country tracks also deviate. Crows do not circle like hawks catching thermals in a vortex of their own, rising, falling, suddenly swooping off course for a tasty rodent that has rashly exposed itself. They do not fly in a V like geese, suggesting perfect formation, but really even geese shift and scatter, replace each other in line, now follow, now lead. Crows don't circle or V. Nor do they bisect the sky with a cleaver. They have their detours, their distractions, their disruptions between departure and arrival. Like ambitious mothers with aspirations, they get preoccupied with the dailiness of feeding and preening, breeding and nesting. Destinations are postponed, cancelled for another season. Even migration is waning in the nineties and the noughts with more birds staying all winter in the warmer weather.

I've seen swans follow roadways, tour the highway each spring in search of the cold tundra, taking the curves with the cars. Small planes do this too, use the roads as their guide. Or they fly over huge hydro corridors gouged diagonally out of the land to carry juice from heavy blue-water generators on sunset beaches to the big smoke of the city. Flyers spend their Sundays above the high wires, without a net, trading neon lights for the view of a straight swath that has been tamed and sprayed with toxic chemicals and toxic rays. On damp days the hydro lines sing and buzz, and a baby's pram wheeled beneath them will vibrate, metal moving metal, energizing more than the lines. Kids grow big here. And tall. And quickly too.

Hydro helicopters follow the corridor looking for problems or leaks, for spare electricity escaping into the atmosphere. And damage comes from the energy they attract as well as convey, for lightning loves them and forks jagged nails into the towers like divine fingers, galvanizing the hot symmetry of the line. But only ice makes them crumple and fall.

Police helicopters look for dope in the fields, thick plants concealed in caches and creek beds. Choppers check the corn rows, following lines of their own over backwoods, riverbanks and clearings, flying low so others won't get high.

Herons fly from pond to pond, their enormous bodies reduced to floating down, their doubled necks folded like garment bags to carry on, their claws pointed as rudders. Their wings span an adult's arms and cup the air at the low pace of the metronome. Slowly, with purpose. A Mahler adagio. No wasted move. But the hydro lines transect the ponds. Impose an unnatural barrier at just the wrong height. And the herons notice late, swerve, bank, fluster and dive. They return to rethink their plan, re-navigate their altitude, their path. Where hawks land, herons falter. They are not linesbirds.

Starlings travel in a ribbon. They fly a fickle path, turning the strand inside out and over and down, up and around. Migrating noisemakers, they fill trees at night, squawk at dusk, queue on wires at dawn, gossiping. Don't hang your laundry out on starling days. Particularly if there are wild grapes and chokecherries in the fencerows. One flyby stains purple.

WHEN I WALK through a wet wood or field to the magic beech, the corduroy road or the watercress and double home on my tracks, I can see the folly of my straight intentions. There is no crow's line here, no level, no plumb, no transit. My path hedges and falters around the groundhog holes (front and back doors— some with carports), the odd thistle or burdock. It swerves to investigate a plant or a bug, shifts in direction with the whim of the moment.

There is so much to see. And why not be waylaid? The pussy toes have grown to whole feet. The goldenrod flush in full payoff. The chicory reflects the sky. Alfalfa blooms purple and mauve again, and some late clover grows alongside the shrivelled heads of flowers past. Queen Anne's lace is ruffed around a rich murex centre big enough only for the vase of the smallest sprite. Haws hide the thorns. Apples are yellow and red, striped and russet.

I walk in a wavy line, a path I create anew each time,

or follow one side of the tractor trail. Until I realize it is taking me elsewhere, away from my destination. Such is the draw of a path. In planted fields I walk on the edge. Must not damage the crop. But the edges are rough, grown over and perilously close to the ploughed trough. In a harvested field nothing can be hurt, but still my inclination is to keep to the verge or walk in the rows imposed by machinery. By humanity's need to control, to order, to straighten curves.

On summer walks, fresh cow pats fester in the neighbour's fields. The shit-flies, large amber insects, ironically fragile and filigreed, work steadily, taking what they need and leaving the nitrogen for the field. But while they tread softly on top, delicately doing their salvage work, I will sink in, squish and slide and carry cow pie with me over the hill. So these too must be seen and swerved for. Sheep scat, pelleted and solid, is more forgiving, but it finds the cracks in my boots and lodges there, content to see the world from dark to dark, tread to tread.

Tracks signal a journey. Only the trekker can decide whether the journey surpasses the destination. Walking in the wild commands all the senses, the gross and the delicate. Wide eyes absorb the vistas and fine focus catches the details. The elm, survivor of decimating disease, despite its Dutch stewards, stands alone on a crest and is a surprise every time. It rises from the planted earth like a cairn to loss. A sole specimen of a noble race. But if my eyes hug the path to help my feet dodge the tripsters and

pitfalls, I can miss it. I can scurry right by without notic-
ing. And how few of us even know it is there?

I am a walker, not a maker, of paths. There are those
who obsess with cutting the swath, while I am content to
follow on foot, on skis, or snowshoes. As a child I
watched my grandfather's hired man, Harvey, with his
machete. He'd cut and clear miles and miles of paths
from cottage to boathouse, cottage to bathhouse, ice
house to woodshed, and all around a northern shoreline
too long for me to walk in a day. He carved magic paths
just beside the water, over granite and through raspberries, exposing gnarled roots of yellow birch spread
like giant atrophied fingers over rocks and moss. His
paths revealed fungus to draw on, lichen to dye with, win-
tergreen for tea and moss for pillows. Every kind of maple
and ironwood and birch. Cedars, white and Jack pine,
red oak, hemlock and balsam. And so many ferns. The
only way to see that wood was through his paths, or by
paddling close to the shore and peering in. But underbrush conceals and canoes follow paths of their own.

The first time I took Thomas to that place I led him
away from the road, along a mile of sandy gravel lane,
which had been laid so many years ago. We struck for the
path through the woods to see this place together, to
walk on the soft needle carpet.

Harvey was gone by then, as well as my grandfather,
who had lorded over that land. And to my horror, so
was the path—all of the paths. They'd grown over in a

season, relentlessly filling in. Unused and unbrushed. Thomas felt my sorrow, surpassed my skill. He took up the machete, and the paths, one by one, reappeared. Now my daughter, tools in hand, heads back to continue that work, follow the legacy and create her own corner in that land of our blood. And her brother will join her with his own clearing tools.

OUR SON has tracks of his own. Single track, close-clipped and tirelessly thrashed, designed for danger and thrill and speed. Tracks for mountain bikes and snowboards. Tracks with hairpin turns and jumps. Tracks that need constant attention, cutting and brushing, brushing and cutting.

My father made tractor tracks in his woods. Drew out more logs than his fireplace could ever burn. Made whole summers of tracks, whole winters of wood. The sound of the Ford 8N, which lives here now, the sound of the chainsaw. If the neighbours miss my dad, I doubt they miss that noise. While fishers trolled quietly and bathers sunned, he took on the forest. Tamed it with his trails, his fluorescent tape and iron stakes. Each morning he put a nickel on the map of the land so my mother would know where to look if he didn't return. And she said to me, "I never would."

WINTER TRAILS leave less room for meandering or independence. Whoever breaks the trail gets to choose the way—that slogging work has its reward. Single tracks double in the snow. Two skis, side by side, imprint the way.

Coons leave their nailprints by the river, and dogs dicker in the mud. But I've never seen a fox track in anything but snow. And nothing is so distinctive. One small foot in front of another and another. A straight line of feet with few diversions. Foxes know where they are going. Purposeful A-to-B creatures. Straight as crows.

Rabbits, silly ziggers and zaggers, are so busy in snow that their tracks turn to half-pipes, patterned over and over with lucky footprints, like the path of a giant mole with its roof removed for study. So busy, these bunnies, backing and forthing between brush piles and tree roots, bringing the news from there to here and taking it back again. The ants of winter.

Other snow tracks are harder to read. The soft marks of birds fluffed on perches or the minute snow angels formed by flying and landing, spaced at odd intervals. Only the imprint of the wingfeathers or a tail gives them away. A ruffed grouse, bobwhite, or blue jay pausing. Or a jumping mouse, who leaves ridiculously far-fetched spaces between landings, little holes in loose powder, with tail-lines behind. As if some sky creature reached down to make a pattern in the snow for its own amusement, using the field as a celestial board game.

Summer smells of sweet hay and honeysuckle give way to rank dew and leaf mould, scent of late asters and fermenting fall berries, then winter crispness freezes nostrils. Only the crumple of evergreen underfoot perfumes the air. Woodsmoke rises from the farm-house until March, when it mingles with the sappy smell of maple burning and boiling, as syrup bubbles in the cauldron. Circular sugar tracks lead in a maze of sidesteps to individual trees that give up their bounty in a lachrymose labour. The full sun triggers a steady stream of sap, but in the cold and grey, the maples close their eyes in dormancy. The snow track becomes mud mixed with rotting forest floor. My big black boot heels wedge their stamped rubber maple leaf pattern into the real thing under each tap. And even the rabbits must wonder at a path with so many turns, so little distance, filled with the baby steps of Mother May I, necessitated by carrying a bucket growing ever heavier with sap.

CROWS FLY in curves. We carve or careen, make tracks straight or crooked, or follow the undulations of the moment, never stepping on the same ground twice. Like water, the earth, rock and plants morph with time, and as we are changed from day to day, so they alter, atom by atom, ever recreating the path, the destination and the quest.

⊰ *BUS BUST* ⊱

⌇ AS THE GROUND CHANGES and the season changes, so do the faces I see at my morning table each day. They change ever so slowly, moving from the crook of my arms to the raised cane chair to the booster seat to the pressback, until suddenly they are grown, they are going, they are gone. And the familiar face left is crowned in grey. It has lines now, mirroring my own.

The hands that move over the table have changed too. From the first grip with chubby palms, the first grasp of spoon or crayon, the first fist of displeasure, to the expressive movements of creative thought, the manual illustration of rational thinking, the cursive writing, the keyboard tapping, the filling in of applications and forms, the tentative opening of mail announcing acceptances, scholarships and imminent departures. And the hands left behind have callouses and veins and tracks leading from all the elements of this place. Scars and memories of the thorns and nails, the softest down of newborn children and lambs, the bites of hay and brambles and the lashes of wire and stone, the knowledge of countless skills. And still the hands fold on my table. Our table. And reach across to each other.

The quest—that need to discover this land, to learn to create, to steward our piece of earth—stays with me, with us. But the players age, they grow, and suddenly we find ourselves back to the number we started with. Just two. The children we never even dreamed of when we first came here are now setting off on their own.

The bus still travels our road. It's a tad later now that it doesn't have to stop here, and it goes by a lot faster. I don't miss marking my day by its schedule. Sometimes I see it from my bed while lying barely awake, or reading, my tea steaming in its mug. No more wake-up calls, packing lunches, doing last-minute laundry. I do not miss those stresses, though the void they leave is filled by other holes, tiny vials of blank space, tiny vacuums pulling part of me, tugging gently, relentlessly.

WE HAD a number of bus drivers over the years. The religious, the righteous, the reverser, the hunter who craned for deer every fall. They broke down, got stuck, got ornery, got stubborn and got my kids safely to school and back, and they were saints to do it. At the start we were cautioned that the children might have to walk to the corner, not too far, but along a hilly gravel road where pickups travel too fast. I would not have been able to watch them waiting at that corner, nor shelter them, nor trust in their safety, but it never happened. The bus always came to the lane. The ancient maple was threatened when it prevented one driver from turning the bus. But it just presented a challenge to another, who would simply back up to the door. The gift of reverse. The bus still goes by and the maple remains, though it loses limbs in each storm and its crown grows thinner each summer. The tree stands, shades, shelters and safeguards this place like a sentry.

The bus house, which saw small children enter its door, peer up at its back window and press noses on its front one, housed my daughter and son through elementary and high school. It housed more and more items as more of its space was taken up by the children's growth: mouse nests, fossils, a collection of rocks and papers too important to pitch away. In bad weather I could watch from the kitchen on days when even the dog wouldn't venture down the lane. My kids would be blown sideways, hands to their hoods, lunch boxes flapping against their thighs as they disappeared altogether in a sudden whiteout. They would gingerly open the door of the shelter, scramble inside and close themselves in, fogging the glass with their breath.

On snowy days the bus is difficult to hear. Its hard wheels roll on soft roads, often making the first track of the day. I would know it was coming only by seeing the children emerge from their house, stop to latch the door so it wouldn't blow open and away, then turn to meet the bus pulling up, its lights flashing, its rat-trap colour glowing.

At the end of the day I would await its return and watch the children jump off or sometimes trail off, dragging their stuff. They would run or saunter, heads up or down, depending on their day. My daughter would chatter to her brother, who tended to be taciturn. She was energized by the ride while he was subdued. Or sometimes the reverse. They'd bring me the news of their lives. Or not.

They avoided the bus house after school, though occasionally I saw them stow something inside, stash it for later retrieval perhaps. Or for protection from censure. The building soon became a fixture, stained pale green, blending with the grass and the trees, its greyish-brown door in tone with the shingles, camouflaged with the stone wall that went up beside it, the gate built behind it, the gravel of the road it bordered, the lane.

At first incongruous, the house's height eventually made sense as my son grew and grew to six foot six. And how, I wonder, did Thomas know he would get so tall? Perhaps through the formula of prediction that doubles the height of a two-year-old, or is it a three-year-old? That code could have been a hint, but we live by science here, not tales. Or do we?

Science and nature and nurture and history.
Community and wisdom and education and knowledge.
Skill and intuition. Earth in the blood, like bagpipes.
You have it or you don't. Precognition and synesthesia.
And just plain knowing. Or guessing. Or acting on a
hunch. These are all things we garner while living here.
And the outsized bus house, which reached farther into
the atmosphere than anyone could expect a child to
grow, proved perfect in the end. When I checked the
door frame in the mudroom with my metal tape, I was
astonished to find it exactly right. At three he was exactly half of six-and-a-half-feet high.

Before he grew so tall the bus house provided him
with a step on the way into the maple tree beside it.
He'd climb from the fence to the roof of the bus house
to the thick branch and on up to the trunk of the tree
and beyond, as high as high. It was his solitary place
above us all, where he got ready to suffer heights for the
rest of his life. One day he went farther, higher perhaps, and he could not get down. His father got the
extension ladder and went up after him. Never,
Thomas told him, is it wrong to ask for help, to accept
rescue, to admit your limits. There is no cowardice in
safety. A lesson I hope he will always retain.

Over the years the bus house weathered. The glass
was broken when boys made a swift exit from the roof;
the paint on the door peeled. The mice moved in. The
chairs disappeared. They were stripped and refinished,

repaired and reglued and taken to live in the city with my daughter.

One spring, during the final final exams, the bus made its last stop, its last pause since its first all those years ago for a swimming lesson. And shortly after, my son and Thomas, men together, decided to take the bus house away, move it on to a different spot, a different life. They took off the door, put the house on tilt, tried to perch it on the trailer to move it, but it defeated them. Too big, too heavy, too stubborn to leave, it lay stuck in the lane, upended, rugged, determined and stationary.

It wasn't long before the flying Dutchman—*de vliegende Hollander*—arrived, by fate, by luck, by his innate skill at knowing when he's needed most. With the front-end loader at the ready, and skill and daring ever present, he gently tipped the house into the bucket, tilted it just so, and took it down through the Meadow, along by the Swamp, through Knock-down Corner and into the sugar bush. Together they set it back up, put stones beneath the corners, turned it at an angle and settled it in to its new work in the woods. It no longer harbours children each morning, stores their treasures at night or witnesses the to-ing and fro-ing of the bus. Retired as a bus house, it awaits rebirth in March, when the sap begins to run and the fires start to burn under the kettle. It will keep our equipment safe and dry, give us shelter in the sugar bush, remind us of the shifting stages of our lives here in this place.

So I look out my kitchen window and see the stone wall, the gate beside it, see the cedar hedge, the gravel lane and the maple tree. The bus house is gone, as if it had never been there. But like the children it sheltered, it lives on in a new place with a new life. Its future lies before it like a well-loved carpet that has been gathered up gently and freshly rolled.

⤙ *DAGS* ⤚

⫷ THE WINTER HAS BEEN BITTER this year. We've had storm after storm, grey upon grey, snow and sleet and treacherous conditions. The roads have been closed, the winds cruel and the sun scarce. The days are creeping longer, but spring is hiding in a maze, not perching around a corner.

I think about endings. About my children leaving home, about my book's last pages, about my youth paid out and spent here on the farm. All the disjunctions and connections, trajectories bleeding off into the distance and circles meeting up. Continua humming like cicadas, which sound like singing wires, taut and vibrating. Intersecting lines travelling at their own speeds and following divergent courses, but meeting for a moment. A brief kiss in one place, a small dot of focus.

So much of what I do here is contradictory. Sheltering and slaughtering. Planting and harvesting.

Conservation and consumption. Solitude and community. But perhaps that's exactly what this life is, a delicate balance of disparate and warring concepts, brief moments of harmony in the dissonance of nature and culture.

Lambsquarters is a snug harbour for its animals. The sick and the wounded are sheltered within its gates. Helen, daft lamb that she was, wouldn't have survived in other barns. But here she was cherished, nurtured and coddled into her limited life. Her enthusiasm and tenacity carried her along after our hand-rearing was finished. Eventually I did get to the fleece that we carefully removed from her cooling skin the day she died in the barnyard. It took me some time. But for the last Christmas of the century I carded and spun it and formed the necks of sweaters for my children and their father. Like the Victorians who wore jewellery woven with the hair of the dearly departed, my beloveds wear Helen's wool around their necks. Helen was knit into their lives first as a lamb and then into their sweaters. And on my needles is a cardigan whose collar will be Helen as well. That lamb who warmed my heart will warm me again. A mourning cloak. She's a legend, my Helen, living still in a poem by a friend. There's a good chance she would be in the flock still, had she not been afflicted. But her brother went for slaughter, as do most of the rams. And how can I justify that contradiction? The ways of the farm. The lives of animals who would never exist but for their value as meat and wool.

I PLANT MY GARDENS with tender touch, urge seeds along in the house, transplant them on dusky days, protect them from too much sun, from predators, from drought. But just when they reach adulthood I rip them down, steal their fruit, bouquet their blossoms, dig their roots. I am self-serving with my gardens, hacking out what doesn't blend, what doesn't taste, what doesn't suit my current design. I train ground lovers to entwine upwards, prune tomatoes to increase production, pinch flowers to amass their blooms. And the weeds better watch out. I show no mercy.

I conserve my land, keep it growing, but consume it as well. There is little summer fallow around here anymore. Every acre grows every year. I love the wild but hate the burdock. I appreciate the brilliant Scotch thistle but hack it down as inedible, prickly, insidious. How does that fit with conservation? I save my dead-head flower seeds every year, sprinkle them on the roadsides that someone else trims. They proclaim their survival with glorious bloom, yet are weeds to the crops if they slip from the ditch.

Trying to be conscious of the needs of the farmers, the constant push to increase production and make the life pay, I acquiesce to the stockpiling of manure across the road, to the widening of the lane for access. But I ask for the plan, question the practice. We compromise. Some trees go, but not all. I still have my view, my borrowed landscape, my precious cedars that house all manner of songbirds. But I will never know how this places me with my neighbours. Their concerns are so different from mine.

I LOVE the solitude of life without houses in sight, yet I crave community at times and feel blessed with the village down the road, the way dotted with barns and houses containing lives connected to each other and my own. The sparse winter necklace of scarce and precious lights spread out on an invisible thread into the distance of the night. There is freedom in the space here, the open vistas and expanses, the tight forests and arcades. I can go for days without seeing anyone else, just the faint view of the odd vehicle on the snowy road, a vision that summer leaves obscure.

But the isolation can be frightening at times. On my first summer night alone in the house there were thunking noises repeated over and over near the window. The fear of investigating fought with the need to know. Who was out there? What was happening? I crept closer, lights out, and watched small apples, one after another, drop from the tree to the ground, bounce and roll away on the grass.

I remember the night when a tractor from the barren east drove into the lane, pulled up by the barn, turned off and stayed in the dark. Nothing else happened. No knock on the door. Nothing. We had puppies for sale, Zoë's litter mates. We had put up a crude sign at the road, and a gentle neighbour (developmentally delayed) had come to pick one out. He always stayed outside until greeted, yet how was I to know that then? The longer he remained out in the dark, the fiercer my imagination. I envisioned phone wires cut, weapons glistening. I telephoned the flying Dutchman, who chuckled, and rushed over while I stood in an upstairs window waiting and watching for him. And still I fretted, for after he had arrived no one came to the house. Only when the tractor left did I hear the story of the man. He returned the next day to pick his pup, and both of us were happy with the transaction.

I've been worried by visiting evangelists, who catch me in the garden where I have no escape. I've given eggs to tramps who've walked in from nowhere. I've held tight to my hoe in the presence of an aggressive salesman and followed my intuition more than once. I listen to my body when it bristles. And I've been known to hide in the barn or to bring the axe inside the house on occasion.

Countering these moments of fear with strangers are the moments of care from the community. The door-to-door collections when someone dies. The cards of thanks. The inevitable help that follows trouble. The gifts of food and flowers, eggs and vegetables. The rides to the hospital, tows from the ditch, boosts of batteries, help with chores and the sharing of all the knowledge there is. As constant as cream rising. Alderney cream.

IN GREY COUNTY there is brutality and gentleness, side by side. There are constant binaries of black and white. Bluebirds and cardinals, siskins and finches. Chickadees sleeping with their heads perched under wing and phoebes nesting in doorways. Crows kidnapping robins' fledglings. Cowbird cuckoos pushing eggs out of nests. Blue jays ravishing hatchlings. The predators and the prey, side by side, all within view.

A sharp-shinned hawk, splendid, slate-backed, with rufous breast in bars, *accipiter striatus velox* (Blue Darter to those who know it well) spent a day on the apple tree this late winter. Right beside the house. Right over the bird feeder. Not interested in seeds, it froze on its perch, its feathers impervious to the winds whipping by. Its red eyes were wide and nothing moved but its neck, which seemed to swing completely round, keeping its prey in view. I was struck by its majesty, that Hughesian conceit, creation in its foot. I was mesmerized by its presence, by its purpose and plan.

I could have frightened it, made noise, opened the door. But I watched, transfixed, as it eyed the small oblivious herbivores below. I was implicated in its crime, for I knew and did nothing. The hawk took its time, sized up the perfect kill, the perfect meal. Just when I thought nothing would happen it swooped, clasped a sparrow in its talons and held the bug-eyed birdlet to the ground, smothering in the grasp. Too late I banged the door, hoping it would drop its prey, fly away. Hoping I could be witness and judge both, view the catch and prevent the kill. But there is no such power here. I thwart or I watch.

The hawk heard me. It spread its wings and rose, leaving angel patterns in the snow, holding the sparrow firmly in those thin feet on shapely legs. The hawk took its prey to the cedars beside the house, balanced on a crotch in a branch and tore off its head. Eating it whole. Down through the body it hooked the flesh and ate, small feathers flying in the wind. Not a bone dropped. Not a drop of blood. It took an hour for the hawk, its feet and beak red, to finish. Nothing was wasted, nothing left.

IT SEEMS spring will never come, that the snow will never go as the children, who are no longer children, go back to their lives in separate cities after their holiday. We return from the bus stop, the airport, and Sydney runs up to lick our hands. The sheep call from the barn to be fed. Frontenac and Lanark purr their pleasure when we reach the feed room.

Chores done, we stroll back together to an empty house. Now calm and still, the bustle of a full family stretched out behind us. The house we had never meant to fill. We enter the warm yellow light of the kitchen, fighting the emptiness, the empty nest, and something stirs on the floor. I look closely and find a butterfly. In winter.

Attenuating then slowly draping its wings, it sits on

the maple floorboard, bewildered. Some chrysalis somewhere, on a plant I brought in months before, must be shrivelling and falling apart, breaking to dust. The female lepidopterous *Artogeia rapae*, small white, is out of its cocoon too soon. It's a sign of spring, of hope, of rebirth. A sign of metamorphosis in brilliant yellow and white with velvet black spots.

OUR METHODS are different and our resources more varied, but the vision that spirited us here carries ghosts from the past. Our ancestors, like those of our neighbours, pioneered the land, just not in this place. Their lives course through our veins from pre-memory. The first moment we saw this property that dreams are made on, we knew it was the place we would steward and carefully guard. Made up of woods and fields, hills and valleys, swamp and dry land, its history is a vast effort of human hope, labour, tenacity, frustration and love, and would be protected and nurtured in our still learning hands. We are growing old here.

The wind freshens. A gust shivers across the loose snow and scatters a handful of flakes. They land in a flower bed, are caught by a crinkled leaf wintered brown and rotting. With another rush the leaf shifts, flakes flicking, and lifts, falters, waves farewell and sails away. A single flower, a nodding snowdrop, shelters there pushing its way up from the bulb in the depths, announcing spring.

ACKNOWLEDGEMENTS

To Annie Garton, Cathy Huntley, Don Mason and Anna Sonser for helping me reread the farm so I could write it; to Denise Bukowski and Anne Collins for spinning the text into type; to Esta Spalding, Janice Kulyk Keefer and the late Libby Scheier for literary guidance; to the van Zoelens, the Lewises and the Aitkens for their generosity and their wisdom; and to Connie and Leon Rooke, my first readers, my enthusiasts, my mentors.